Praise for *Be Creative - Now!*

'Rawling's book is succinct, ... and profoundly useful. His thoughtful text sits squarely in the "read again" section of my library!'

Professor Phil Manning, College of Charleston (USA) and University of Manchester (UK)

'A never-ending toolkit of creative approaches to whatever challenges you or your business are facing. Brilliant and useful.'

Sam Lewens, Creative Director and TV Executive Producer

'All you need to know in management! The perfect toolkit for managers in the millennium.'

Rose Marley, CEO, SharpFutures Manchester

'Takes you on an exciting journey that leaves you making better, impressive and more creative ideas than your competitors. Use these tools and exercises either as a team, or keep them as your little secret.'

Andy Mayer, Director of Strategy, Yoomee Digital

Be Creative – Now!

PEARSON

At Pearson, we believe in learning – all kinds of learning for all kinds of people. Whether it's at home, in the classroom or in the workplace, learning is the key to improving our life chances.

That's why we're working with leading authors to bring you the latest thinking and best practices, so you can get better at the things that are important to you. You can learn on the page or on the move, and with content that's always crafted to help you understand quickly and apply what you've learned.

If you want to upgrade your personal skills or accelerate your career, become a more effective leader or more powerful communicator, discover new opportunities or simply find more inspiration, we can help you make progress in your work and life.

Every day our work helps learning flourish, and wherever learning flourishes, so do people.

To learn more, please visit us at **www.pearson.com/uk**

Be Creative – Now!

The 2-in-1 Manager: Speed Read – instant tips; Big Picture – lasting results

Steve Rawling

PEARSON

Harlow, England • London • New York • Boston • San Francisco • Toronto • Sydney
Auckland • Singapore • Hong Kong • Tokyo • Seoul • Taipei • New Delhi
Cape Town • São Paulo • Mexico City • Madrid • Amsterdam • Munich • Paris • Milan

Pearson Education Limited
Edinburgh Gate
Harlow CM20 2JE
United Kingdom
Tel: +44 (0)1279 623623
Web: www.pearson.com/uk

First published 2016 (print and electronic)

© Steve Rawling 2016 (print and electronic)

The right of Steve Rawling to be identified as author of this work has been asserted by him in accordance with the Copyright, Designs and Patents Act 1988.

Pearson Education is not responsible for the content of third-party internet sites.

ISBN: 978-1-292-11929-8 (print)
 978-1-292-11931-1 (PDF)
 978-1-292-11932-8 (ePub)

British Library Cataloguing-in-Publication Data
A catalogue record for the print edition is available from the British Library

Library of Congress Cataloging-in-Publication Data
Names: Rawling, Steve, author.
Title: Be creative - now! : the 2-in-1 manager : speed read--instant tips, big picture–lasting results / Steve Rawling.
Description: Harlow, England ; New York : Pearson Education, 2016. | Includes bibliographical references and index.
Identifiers: LCCN 2016001150| ISBN 9781292119298 (print) | ISBN 9781292119311 (pdf)
Subjects: LCSH: Creative thinking. | Creative ability in business. | Problem solving. | Creative ability.
Classification: LCC HD53 .R377 2016 | DDC 650.1--dc23
LC record available at http://lccn.loc.gov/2016001150

The print publication is protected by copyright. Prior to any prohibited reproduction, storage in a retrieval system, distribution or transmission in any form or by any means, electronic, mechanical, recording or otherwise, permission should be obtained from the publisher or, where applicable, a licence permitting restricted copying in the United Kingdom should be obtained from the Copyright Licensing Agency Ltd, Barnard's Inn, 86 Fetter Lane, London EC4A 1EN.

The ePublication is protected by copyright and must not be copied, reproduced, transferred, distributed, leased, licensed or publicly performed or used in any way except as specifically permitted in writing by the publishers, as allowed under the terms and conditions under which it was purchased, or as strictly permitted by applicable copyright law. Any unauthorised distribution or use of this text may be a direct infringement of the author's and the publishers' rights and those responsible may be liable in law accordingly.

All trademarks used herein are the property of their respective owners. The use of any trademark in this text does not vest in the author or publisher any trademark ownership rights in such trademarks, nor does the use of such trademarks imply any affiliation with or endorsement of this book by such owners.

Contains public sector information licensed under the Open Government Licence (OGL) v3.0. http://www.nationalarchives.gov.uk/doc/open-government-licence/version/3/

10 9 8 7 6 5 4 3 2 1
20 19 18 17 16

Cover design by Two Associates

Print edition typeset in 10pt Scene Std by SPi Global
Print edition printed in Great Britain by Henry Ling Ltd, at the Dorset Press, Dorchester, Dorset

NOTE THAT ANY PAGE CROSS REFERENCES REFER TO THE PRINT EDITION

Contents

About the author xiii
Acknowledgements xiv
How to use this book xvi

Chapter 1 BE MORE CREATIVE 1

Speed read 3
1.1 Defeat habit with originality 3
1.2 Divergent thinking 4
1.3 Lateral thinking 5
1.4 Convergent thinking 6
1.5 Time and space 7
1.6 Group dynamics 8
1.7 Choose the right tools for the job 9

Big picture 11
1.1 Defeat habit with originality 11
1.2 Divergent thinking 14
1.3 Lateral thinking 17
1.4 Convergent thinking 20
1.5 Time and space 25

Contents

   1.6 Group dynamics   27
   1.7 Choose the right tools for the job   31

Chapter 2 YOUR CREATIVE MISSION   33

Speed read   35

   2.1 Imagine a world without you   35
   2.2 Apply the power of why   36
   2.3 What's your problem?   36
   2.4 The lizard, the chimp and the business exec   37
   2.5 Four ways of seeing   38
   2.6 Give and take   38
   2.7 Tweet simplicity   39

Big picture   41

   2.1 Imagine a world without you   41
   2.2 Apply the power of why   44
   2.3 What's your problem?   47
   2.4 The lizard, the chimp and the business exec   51
   2.5 Four ways of seeing   54
   2.6 Give and take   56
   2.7 Tweet simplicity   60

Chapter 3 INSIGHTS AND HOOKS   65

Speed read   67

   3.1 That's funny …   67
   3.2 Burst your filter bubble   68

3.3	Make connections	69
3.4	Use contradictions	70
3.5	Field trips and freshness stores	71
3.6	What's my motivation?	72
3.7	Crafting a compelling hook	73

Big picture 75

3.1	That's funny ...	75
3.2	Burst your filter bubble	78
3.3	Make connections	82
3.4	Use contradictions	84
3.5	Field trips and freshness stores	89
3.6	What's my motivation?	94
3.7	Crafting a compelling hook	98

Chapter 4 FORCED INSPIRATION 103

Speed read 105

4.1	Brainstorm rules	105
4.2	The lateral nudge and metaphor mash	106
4.3	Mapping your thoughts	107
4.4	Steal from the heart	108
4.5	Break the rules	109
4.6	Look harder inside the box	110
4.7	Brainwriting tools	110

Contents

Big picture   113

    4.1   Brainstorm rules   113
    4.2   The lateral nudge and metaphor mash   116
    4.3   Mapping your thoughts   120
    4.4   Steal from the heart   125
    4.5   Break the rules   129
    4.6   Look harder inside the box   133
    4.7   Brainwriting tools   138

Chapter 5   NURTURE GOOD IDEAS   143

Speed read   145

    5.1   The developer's dilemma   145
    5.2   Supportive teams   146
    5.3   Widen your pool of talent   147
    5.4   Design thinking   147
    5.5   Keep the novelty alive   148
    5.6   Working with wild ideas   149
    5.7   Moving out of the greenhouse   150

Big picture   153

    5.1   The developer's dilemma   153
    5.2   Supportive teams   157
    5.3   Widen your pool of talent   160
    5.4   Design thinking   163
    5.5   Keep the novelty alive   166
    5.6   Working with wild ideas   170
    5.7   Moving out of the greenhouse   174

Chapter 6 WEED OUT BAD IDEAS 179

Speed read 181

6.1 Get serious 181
6.2 The unknown 182
6.3 Groupthink 183
6.4 Optimism bias 183
6.5 Overconfidence 184
6.6 The sunk cost fallacy (aka why it's hard to pull the plug) 185
6.7 How to fail well 186

Big picture 189

6.1 Get serious 189
6.2 The unknown 195
6.3 Groupthink 199
6.4 Optimism bias 202
6.5 Overconfidence 206
6.6 The sunk cost fallacy (aka why it's hard to pull the plug) 209
6.7 How to fail well 215

Chapter 7 SELL YOUR BEST IDEAS 221

Speed read 223

7.1 You, your audience, your message 223
7.2 Real, original, simple 224

7.3	Three is the magic number (and other rhetorical devices)	225
7.4	Go viral	226
7.5	Great stories	227
7.6	Road-test your story	228
7.7	Hand over the spark	229

Big picture — 231

7.1	You, your audience, your message	231
7.2	Real, original, simple	235
7.3	Three is the magic number (and other rhetorical devices)	239
7.4	Go viral	242
7.5	Great stories	246
7.6	Road-test your story	250
7.7	Hand over the spark	253

Index — 257

About the author

Steve Rawling is a former BBC journalist, development producer and trainer. He has spent 20 years in news and documentaries, worked with teams including Drama, Children's, Sport and Natural History and trained on the BBC Academy's Creative Leadership Programme. He is now a freelance trainer and consultant specialising in creative thinking and storytelling.

Acknowledgements

A word of thanks to those who have helped me be more creative. Thanks to Linda Green for setting my feet on a new path. Thanks to Marie Crook for guiding my hand while I wrote this book. Thanks to all the bosses and colleagues who let me try out what I thought were brilliant ideas during a long and enjoyable TV career.

Publisher's acknowledgements

We are grateful to the following for permission to reproduce copyright material:

Figures

Figure on page 21 from Current developments in creative problem solving for organizations: A focus on thinking skills and styles, *The Korean Journal for Thinking and Problem Solving,* 15(2), 43–76 (Puccio, G.J., Murdock, M.C. and Mance, M. 2005); Figure on page 58 adapted from *Gamestorming: A Playbook for Innovators, Rulebreakers and Changemakers,* O'Reilly (Gray, D., Brown, S. and Macanufo, J. 2010) p. 178, Copyright © 2010 Dave Gray, Sunni Brown and James Macanufo; Figures on page 71, 90, 181, 189 and 194 adapted from Traffic Signs Regulations and General Directions 2002, © Crown copyright. Contains public sector information licensed under the Open Government Licence (OGL) v3.0. http://www.nationalarchives.gov.uk/doc/open-government-licence/version/3/; Figure on page 165 from *Targeting: Tool for Evaluation and Group Consensus,* 42nd Annual Creative Problem Solving Institute, New York (Puccio, G.J. and Miller, B. 1996).

Acknowledgements

Tables

Table on page 13 adapted from Defining intolerance of ambiguity, *Psychological Record,* 15(3), 393–400 (Bochner, S. 1965), Copyright © Association for Behavior Analysis International; Table on page 59 adapted from Role ambiguity: A review and integration of the literature, *Journal of Modern Business,* 3, 41–47 (Bauer, J.C. and Simmons, P.R. 2000).

Text

Extract on page 165 from *Targeting: Tool for Evaluation and Group Consensus,* 42nd Annual Creative Problem Solving Institute, New York (Puccio, G.J. and Miller, B. 1996); Extract on pages 254–255 adapted from *Do/Story: How to Tell Your Story so the World Listens,* The Do Book Company (2013), by Bobette Buster, reproduced with permission.

How to use this book

'I'm not very creative . . .'

I've lost count of the times people have said that to me. Maybe you're thinking it as you pick up this book. You don't work in a 'creative' role; you're not a 'creative' type; you keep quiet in ideas meetings because you're 'not very creative'.

Well, I'm not very athletic. But I know if I use certain techniques and work hard, in a few months I will be fitter, stronger and faster. Same goes for creativity.

If you face uncertainty in a changing world, if you need new and useful ways to solve problems, then you need to *Be Creative – Now!* This book has over a hundred tools and exercises to help you:

- generate hundreds – yes, hundreds – of new ideas
- find the most useful ideas among the new ones
- spot bad ideas before they trip you up
- sell your best ideas to others.

Speed read gives you the basics for each chapter and something to do or think about right now.

Big picture goes into detail, explains the thinking behind the chapter and gives you practical tools and exercises to use. Some of these you can do right now in the book, but most of them are designed to be used with groups or teams.

How to use this book

How long have you got?

Some of these techniques work in short bursts. Most take at least half an hour to get the most out of them. You can combine several techniques to take your team through a detailed piece of work over several hours. All the exercise worksheets in this book can be downloaded from www.newthinking.tools.

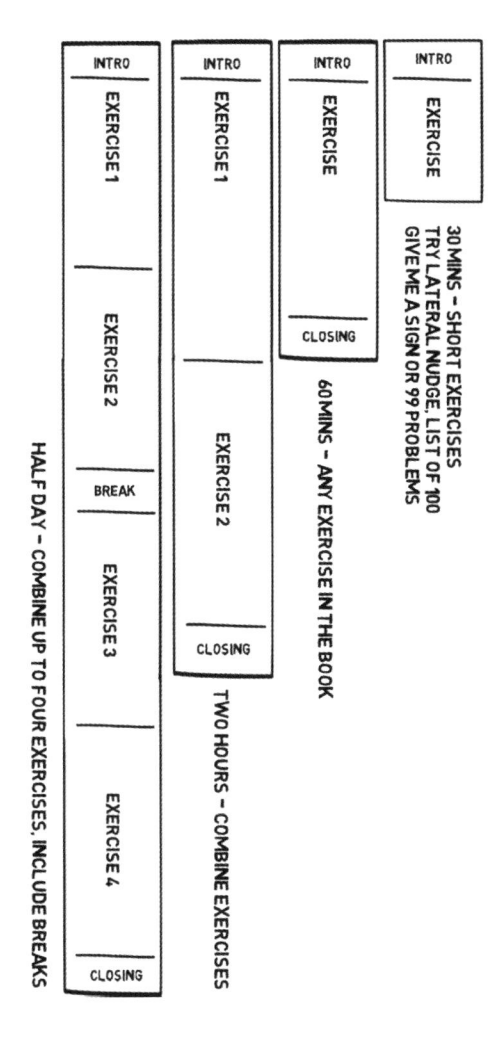

```
HALF DAY – COMBINE UP TO FOUR EXERCISES, INCLUDE BREAKS
  [INTRO | EXERCISE 1 | EXERCISE 2 | BREAK | EXERCISE 3 | EXERCISE 4 | CLOSING]

TWO HOURS – COMBINE EXERCISES
  [INTRO | EXERCISE 1 | EXERCISE 2 | CLOSING]

60 MINS – ANY EXERCISE IN THE BOOK
  [INTRO | EXERCISE | CLOSING]

30 MINS – SHORT EXERCISES
TRY LATERAL NUDGE, LIST OF 100
GIVE ME A SIGN OR 99 PROBLEMS
  [INTRO | EXERCISE]
```

And remember, being creative isn't just a vital career skill – it's also a lot of fun.

Chapter 1

Be more creative

1.1 Defeat habit with originality
1.2 Divergent thinking
1.3 Lateral thinking
1.4 Convergent thinking
1.5 Time and space
1.6 Group dynamics
1.7 Choose the right tools for the job

SPEED READ
1. Be more creative

1.1 Defeat habit with originality

Are you creative?

You don't have to be an artist, a writer or a musician. Creative thinking means finding new ways round problems. We all need it.

So why do we often struggle to come up with new ideas? Whatever our business, we like the tried and tested. It's how we learned our trade and it's how we get things done. But it doesn't take long for habits to form and 'how we did this once' becomes 'how we do things round here'.

Tried and tested can be a barrier to new ideas. Soon you're looking at your rival's new idea and saying, 'I wish I'd thought of that'. This is why you need new thinking tools – for you, your team and your organisation.

> 'I SUPPOSE IT IS TEMPTING, IF THE ONLY TOOL YOU HAVE IS A HAMMER, TO TREAT EVERYTHING AS IF IT WERE A NAIL.'
>
> **ABRAHAM MASLOW**

Any project you work on will need thinkers and do-ers if it's going to succeed. They each bring their own kind of thinking tools to a problem. If you only have do-ers, you'll struggle to break tried and tested habits. If you only have thinkers, you'll struggle to get anything finished.

Be more creative

The tools in this book help do-ers think and help thinkers act. New tools help you find new ideas, weed out bad ideas and sell your best ideas to the people who matter.

You don't want to face a challenging world equipped with only one tool, do you?

> **Do this**
> How creative do you feel? Think of all the problems you've already solved this week. Did they involve finding creative solutions?

1.2 Divergent thinking

Divergent thinking means pushing yourself beyond the obvious answers and first workable solutions. It means generating lots of possible options rather than trying to find one 'right' answer straight away. If you've built a career on fast-reaction decision-making, divergent thinking can feel uncomfortable. But when you push for lots of options, you are much more likely to find novel ideas.

Once you have lots of options in front of you, it's easier to spot connections and common themes – and easier to choose the strongest ideas to take forward.

> **Do this**
> How often do you go with the first workable idea that comes along? How often do you pause and look for other options?

1.3 Lateral thinking

England football manager Sir Bobby Robson used to tell players, 'Practice makes permanent.' This is great advice for an athlete, but *bad* for creative thinkers.

Permanent doesn't help if you need new ways to do something or when the world around you no longer fits the old model. This is when you need new thinking tools.

Our brains have evolved so we can rapidly make sense of a confusing world. They are wonderful pattern-making machines, primed to organise information into categories and sequences. Every time they work, the pattern gets reinforced.

Lateral thinking deliberately tries to break patterns, coming at problems from different angles, starting in unusual places and challenging accepted rules.

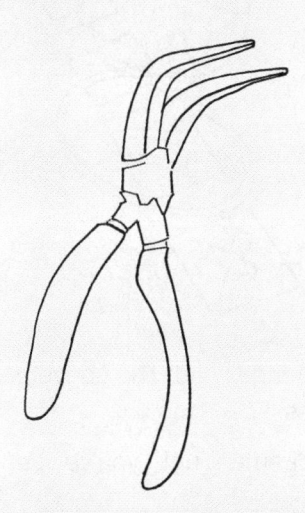

As with divergent thinking, you're trying to find novel options rather than 'right' answers. Again, this can feel uncomfortable at first if you're not used to it.

> **Do this**
> How often do you try to find the 'right' idea straight away? How do you feel about sharing unusual or novel ideas with others?

1.4 Convergent thinking

In an age of massive information overload, most of us are pretty good at narrowing down our options, focusing on what matters and excluding the noise.

This is convergent thinking – taking a wide range of options and selecting the best. In the creative process, convergent thinking follows naturally from a phase of divergent and/or lateral thinking.

There are two challenges with the convergent thinking stage of the creative process:

1. Don't rush to judgement until you've spent time on divergent/lateral thinking.
2. Try to keep the novelty alive from your divergent/lateral thinking.

Do this
Ask yourself how fast you normally move to close down options and choose the best way forward. Do you rush to judgement? How do you feel about keeping options open?

1.5 Time and space

You *cannot* think creatively while sat at your desk, staring at your inbox. You need to carve out time and space for yourself and your team, away from the interruptions and demands of the 'day job'.

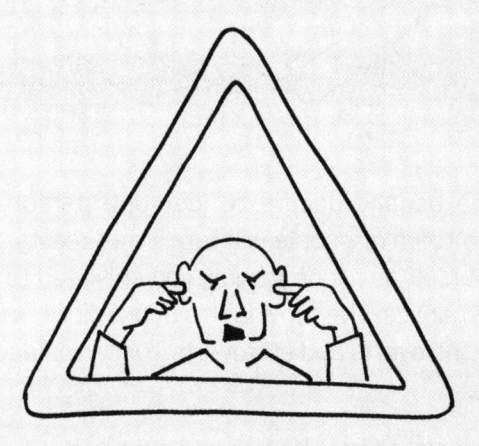

This might mean half an hour or it might be an away-day. Either way, you need to create a different mood in that time and space – where different rules apply. This can be a real challenge. But don't kid yourself – unless you find ways to behave differently you won't be able to think differently.

Do this
Next time you are struggling to solve a problem, get up from your desk and go for a walk. Does a change of scenery make a difference to how you think?

1.6 Group dynamics

Sometimes we need quiet space to think, sometimes it helps to bounce ideas off others. Some people help us think more freely while others put us on our guard.

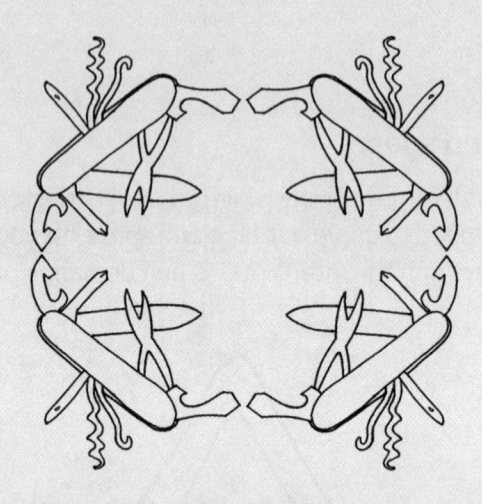

A new idea usually occurs to just one person, but in most situations a team of people will turn it into reality. So even if you think of yourself as a lone genius, you still need to pay attention to group dynamics. The tools in this book will work for groups and individuals, introverts and extroverts, for senior leaders and junior colleagues.

It's always tricky to get the balance right between creativity and discipline in big organisations. As a leader or manager it can be hard to step back and allow creative freedom, especially when deadlines are tight and budgets are tighter. But creative thinking needs autonomy.

Do this
Watch the group dynamics in your workplace. Are there people who encourage sharing of new ideas? Are there people who discourage it? What's the difference in the way they behave?

Speed read

1.7 Choose the right tools for the job

Creative thinking is a process with distinct stages. You've got to know what stage you are at with your project. If you're not sure, you need to work this out by asking the right questions of yourself and others – your colleagues, your boss and your stakeholders. Then choose the right tool for the stage of the process you're at.

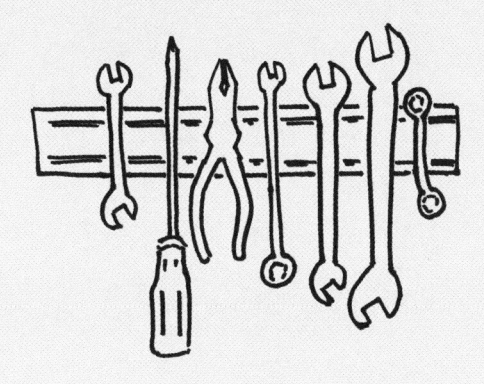

At various points in this book I will refer to 'your project'. This is shorthand for whatever you're working on right now, or would love to work on in the future. You'll get more out of this book if you come at it with a specific project in mind.

> **Do this**
> Describe the project you'd love to make happen. What's the creative problem you're trying to solve? What stage are you at?

BIG PICTURE
1. Be more creative

1.1 Defeat habit with originality

Why

Creative thinking is vital whether you're an artist or in business. It's free, it's fun and it's fulfilling. Sculptures and paintings found in caves show our ancestors were being creative 40,000 years ago.

Creativity is what makes us human. And in business, of course, creative thinking gives you a competitive edge. You can outsource lots of things these days, but you can't afford to outsource ideas.

But why do some people seem so much better at creative thinking than others? It's usually down to a mix of personal thinking preferences and the culture of the place they work. Sometimes these make it easier to be a thinker and sometimes they reward a do-er.

Knowledge briefing

The good news is that creativity is a natural tendency in all of us, although it varies from person to person.

Tolerance of ambiguity is a vital asset in creative thinking. If you can't stand uncertainty, if you prefer having a definite answer over keeping your options open, you will find the process of exploring 'what ifs' frustrating and even unsettling. 'Tolerance of ambiguity will allow individuals to continue to grapple with complex problems, to remain open, and increase the probability of finding a novel solution' (Zenasni et al. 2008).

There are lots of tests for creative thinking, such as the simple 'how many uses can you find for a paper clip?' question (Guilford 1967). Others measure your preference for different stages of the creative process – whether you are a Clarifier, Idea Generator, Developer or Implementer (Grivas and Puccio 2012). And some tell you which way your 'intuitive compass' points, based on your preference for reasoning, playfulness, instinct or achieving results (Cholle 2011).

Most of the tools in this book demand a certain amount of writing. This is because we think in words. When we're stressed by a problem, words run around our heads in endless 'rehearsal loops'. The simple act of writing problems down stops the constant looping and frees up mental space to think. Also, getting a problem down on paper means other people can help you fix it (Levitin 2014).

How

1. Test your tolerance for ambiguity

- Solo exercise, 10–15 minutes.

Answer the questions in the table opposite. If you scored high (above 30), you probably prefer certainty to ambiguity. The forced inspiration tools in Chapter 4 will help you generate lots of new possibilities, although they may feel uncomfortable.

If you scored low (under 30), you're probably happier with ambiguity. The tools for developing good ideas and weeding out bad ones in Chapters 5 and 6 will help you move on from playing with possibilities to making hard decisions.

How strongly do you ...	You might say or think ...	Score 1–10 1 = weak 10 = strong
Feel a need for certainty	I need to know ... Just give me the answer ...	
See most situations as 'black or white'	This is clearly the best option ... That's a terrible idea ...	
Prefer familiar over unfamiliar situations	I'm a bit out of my depth here ... I'm on safe ground now ...	
Reject unusual or different things	This isn't the way we do things ... That's not what I'm used to ...	
Need to find a solution and stick with it	There's got to be an answer ... But we've already decided ...	
Feel the need for early closure	That'll do, let's move on ... Enough discussion, let's act ...	

Source: Adapted from Bochner (1965).

2. Try one of five different online creativity tests on 99u.com

- Solo exercise, 15–30 minutes.
  http://tinyurl.com/5-Creative-Tests

Reflection

Ask your project team-mates to take the same tests. Do they share your creative preferences or not? What could that mean for the way you work together?

References

Bochner, S. (1965) Defining intolerance of ambiguity, *Psychological Record*, 15(3), 393–400.

Cholle, F.P. (2011) *The Intuitive Compass: Why the Best Decisions Balance Reason and Instinct*. Jossey-Bass.

Grivas, C. and Puccio, G. (2012) *The Innovative Team: Unleashing Creative Potential for Breakthrough Results*. Jossey-Bass.

Guilford, J.P. (1967) *The Nature of Human Intelligence*. McGraw-Hill.

Levitin, D.J. (2014) *The Organised Mind: Thinking Straight in an Age of Information Overload*. Penguin Books.

Zenasni, F., Besançon, M. and Lubart, T. (2008) Creativity and tolerance of ambiguity: An empirical study, *The Journal of Creative Behavior*, 42(1), March.

1.2 Divergent thinking

Why

Divergent thinking is a deliberate attempt to come up with lots of options and make them as varied as possible. It assumes that when you're faced with a problem, your obvious ideas tend to come out first. If you need novelty, you have to push on past the predictable. That way you will surprise yourself and others.

Divergent thinking is about trying to find diverse perspectives on a problem rather than looking for the 'right' one. It demands a temporary suspension of the normal rules of decision-making. It may seem like playful or even frivolous behaviour. And you will be tempted to jump on the first workable idea that comes up (see Section 1.4 on convergent thinking).

Knowledge briefing

Divergent thinking is an essential part of the creative process, according to educational theorist Sir Ken Robinson. It means 'the ability to see lots of possible answers to a question' without worrying straight away which is right or wrong. In fact, he argues, 'if you're not prepared to be wrong, you'll never come up with anything original' (Robinson 2006, 2010).

Many writers and artists describe playing around with lots of options before choosing the best one. John Cleese used to create an 'oasis' of uninterrupted time and space (around 90 minutes) for divergent thinking when he was writing for Monty Python. Cleese realised his sketch-writing was more creative than that of his Python colleagues simply because he was willing to play with ideas in the divergent phase for longer than they were (Cleese 2012).

But divergent thinking isn't just an essential skill for writers and artists. Any organisation facing new, complex and difficult problems will benefit if they can harness groups of people who see the world differently: 'Diverse perspectives and tools enable collections of people to find more and better solutions and contribute to overall productivity' (Page 2007).

How

1. Create a special time and space for divergent thinking

What's your equivalent of John Cleese's 90-minute oasis of uninterrupted time and space to play around with ideas?

2. Take a quick divergent thinking test

- Group or solo exercise, 10 minutes.

If you need to convince yourself – or anyone else – of how divergent thinking creates novelty, do this test. Grab a pen and a watch.

Give yourself 60 seconds. Write down as many things as you can that are *orange*...

Time's up. Give yourself another 60 seconds. Keep going.

Reflection

Now count up all the things you wrote. Was the first 'an orange'? That's because, under pressure, obvious ideas come out first.

Emma Coats, Pixar storyboard artist, has this advice for writers: 'Discount the first thing that comes to mind. And the second, third, fourth, fifth – get the obvious out of the way. Surprise yourself' (Coats n.d.). Go back to your list. Where did you surprise yourself? Was it in the first 60 seconds or the last?

Try the orange test on your colleagues. Who finds it easiest to come up with a long list? Whose ideas are most surprising? Do more novel ideas come out the longer they stick at it? Try with different colours: blue – I bet everyone will say 'sky' or 'sea' first; white – snow; red – blood; yellow – sun; green – grass.

References

Cleese, J. (2012) Address to Cannes International Festival of Creativity, 2012. Featured in *Fast Company*: http://tinyurl.com/cleese-creative

Coats, E. (n.d.) *Pixar Rules of Storytelling*: http://tinyurl.com/Pixar-22-Story-Rules

Page, S.E. (2007) *The Difference: How the Power of Diversity Creates Better Groups, Firms, Schools and Societies.* Princeton University Press.

Robinson, K. (2006) Do schools kill creativity? TED Talks.

Robinson, K. (2010) Changing education paradigms. TED Talks: http://tinyurl.com/KenRobinsonLecture

1.3 Lateral thinking

Why

Lateral thinking means coming at familiar problems from different angles. When you start in an unusual place or deliberately break accepted rules, you will shake up settled patterns of thought.

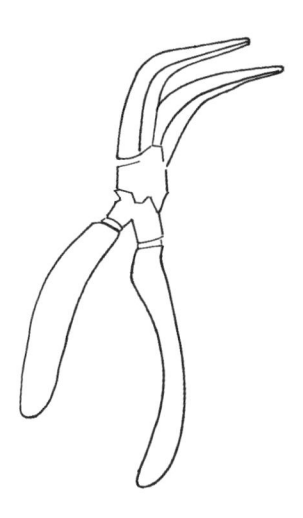

There's one big problem with settled patterns of thought, especially when they keep delivering results. Organisations can fall victim to 'active inertia', responding to threats by doing more of what they do well, rather than trying new approaches.

Innovation means going beyond business as usual. It means coming up with new and improved ideas before your competitors do.

Knowledge briefing

The order in which we receive information affects the way we think about it. We rapidly form patterns which deeply affect our understanding and reasoning about a situation. This is a highly effective way of processing information but keeps us locked into current ways of thinking. Edward de Bono illustrates this by saying: 'You cannot dig a hole in a different place by digging the same hole deeper.' Lateral thinking is a deliberate attempt to distract the brain from its old habits (De Bono 2009; Allan et al. 2002).

For example, based on this personality assessment, would you rather work with Alan or Ben?

Alan	Intelligent – Industrious – Impulsive – Critical – Stubborn – Envious
Ben	Envious – Stubborn – Critical – Impulsive – Industrious – Intelligent

Most people in tests preferred Alan, even though he and Ben *shared identical characteristics.* The order in which they were listed affected our view (Kahneman 2011).

Lateral thinking can seem like an exercise in awkwardness for its own sake, especially if you are challenging patterns which are working just fine. Success encourages us to stick with the tried and tested. Companies can respond to a changing business environment by 'active inertia': in other words, doing more of what worked in the past. They are poorly placed to innovate in fast-changing business environments (Sull 2003).

But hindsight does *not* come with 20:20 vision. We might *think* we know exactly why something succeeded last time, but unless you properly analyse your successes as well as your failures, you could be missing the crucial factor. Your success could be down to something you haven't seen, or just plain luck (Kahneman 2011).

How

1. Test your lateral thinking (2 minutes)

Here are several sequences of letters which belong (in the same order) to a longer word describing a nationality. Work out which nationality each sequence refers to.

Big picture

BRS would be British	ACA would be American
LTV ...	UGD ...
CDI ...	SVK ...
JPS ...	PRV ...
TWN ...	NLH ...

Which one did you find hardest to work out? Was it NLH? So what nationality are the NLH? No, you're not allowed Netherlandish. They're English.

Why was NLH so hard? It's because in every other trio of letters, the first letter was the same as the first letter of the full word. By the tenth trio – NLH – your brain had got into a pattern. So it ran merrily through countries beginning with N, and came up blank.

A lateral thinking – *pattern-breaking* – approach would be to write out gaps *before, in between* and *after* the trio of letters.

  ____ B ____ R ____ S ____ you'd still get British

  ____ N ____ L ____ H ____ you're more likely to get English.

Reflection

Get others around you to take the lateral thinking test. Are you surprised by the results? How hard do you find it to consider new ways of doing something on your project when the old ways seem to be working fine?

References

Allan, D., Kingdon, M., Murrin, K. and Rudkin, D. (2002) *Sticky Wisdom: How to Start a Creative Revolution at Work*. ?WhatIf! Publications.

De Bono, E. (2009) *Lateral Thinking: A Textbook of Creativity*. Penguin Books.

Kahneman, D. (2011) *Thinking, Fast and Slow*. Penguin Books.

Sull, D.N. (2003) *Revival of the Fittest: Why Good Companies Go Bad and How Great Managers Remake*. Harvard Business Press.

1.4 Convergent thinking

Why

Even the greatest thinkers are nothing if they don't move to action. We've all experienced 'analysis-paralysis' when faced with an overwhelming range of options, even something as trivial as which mobile phone to choose.

Most of us find ways around this in our professional lives and become good at convergent thinking. This is the process of narrowing down options, choosing the best and ditching the rest.

In the creative process, this is where it gets real. But the challenge is to converge on the best options while maximising your chances of finding something new and innovative.

Knowledge briefing

Convergent thinking follows on naturally from a phase of divergent or lateral thinking. The first phase generates lots of options, the second phase selects the best options. If you are working in a results-driven environment, you may be under pressure to move to convergent thinking too soon. But if you go with the first workable idea after a short period of divergent thinking (see the diagram below), you never get beyond tried and tested (Puccio et al. 2005).

Big picture

It's worth remembering that most people, when faced with uncertainty, prefer safe options, so you will need to deliberately push them to keep the novelty alive (Mueller *et al.* 2010).

Divergent/convergent model

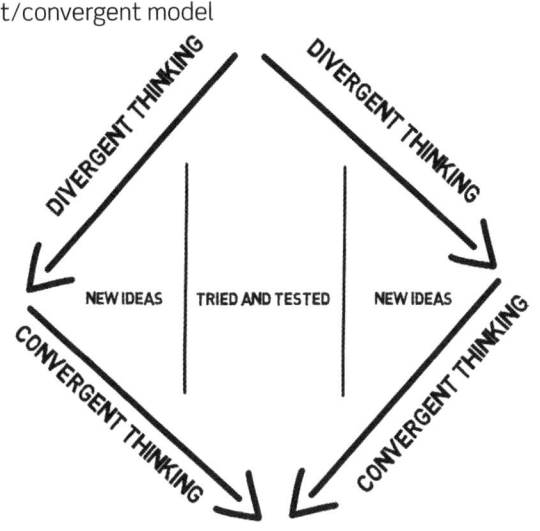

```
         DIVERGENT THINKING        DIVERGENT THINKING
              ↘                          ↙
       NEW IDEAS | TRIED AND TESTED | NEW IDEAS
              ↘                          ↙
         CONVERGENT THINKING       CONVERGENT THINKING
```

Source: From Puccio *et al.* (2005).

In this model, you can see how divergent thinking pushes you further out from the area of familiarity – away from the tried and tested. Only when you have spent time in the area of discovery do you try and find the best ideas.

Lateral thinking helps the divergent phase by starting out in unfamiliar territory.

The authors of *Gamestorming* have a similar model for opening up a discussion and exploring it before closing.

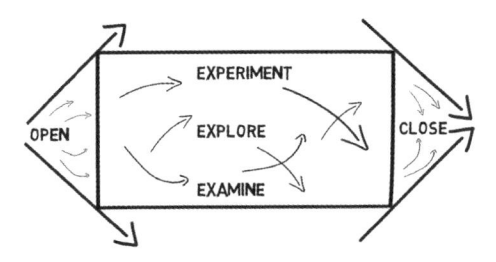

```
              EXPERIMENT
    OPEN   →  EXPLORE    →  CLOSE
              EXAMINE
```

Source: Based on Gray *et al.* (2010).

They have two rules for managing divergent and convergent thinking stages:

- Don't open and close at the same time. They're two different types of thinking. Suspend judgement, stay open-minded, until you're ready to close.
- Close everything you opened. Don't leave options hanging in the air (Gray *et al.* 2010).

How

1. Three little words to stop you converging too soon

If you feel the urge to jump on a workable idea and get straight to action, say out loud:

'Yes, what else?'

It's shorthand for, 'Yep, we could do that and we might come back to that idea, but let's spend a bit more time, see what else we can come up with first, then compare lots of options and pick the best.'

These three little words are your handiest new thinking tool. Get into the habit of saying them over and over again. They are a crowbar for opening minds, dragging yourself and others into the area of discovery.

2. Set a cut-off point for divergent thinking – and don't stop until you hit it

You may be working with sceptics who just don't see the point of brainstorming 'unworkable' ideas. You need to reassure them that the divergent thinking phase will end and be followed by a practical convergent thinking phase. Give it a time limit but *don't* let people stop until you reach it (remember the last 60 seconds in the orange test were more creative than the first).

3. Converge autocratically or democratically – but do it clearly

Faced with a wide range of options, you can converge democratically by asking the group for their favourites. You can

Big picture

do this by discussion or use a dot-voting system and see what patterns emerge.

- List your options.

SIX OPTIONS

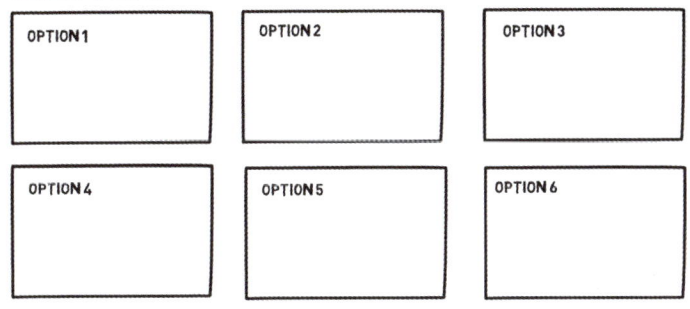

OPTION 1	OPTION 2	OPTION 3
OPTION 4	OPTION 5	OPTION 6

- Give everyone three votes using dots/stickers.

GROUP WITH THREE VOTES EACH

- The option with the most dots is the group's first choice.

SIX OPTIONS

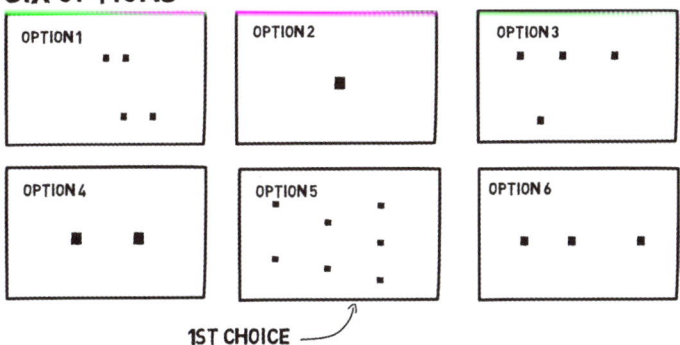

OPTION 1	OPTION 2	OPTION 3
OPTION 4	OPTION 5	OPTION 6

1ST CHOICE

Or you can converge autocratically, by asking the boss/stakeholder to choose their favourite idea. If you signal this clearly in advance, nobody minds. What you *can't* do is ask the group for their choice and then let the boss overrule them.

4. What to say to keep the novelty alive

If you're truly looking for new ideas, keep pushing for novelty at the convergent stage:

- 'Remember, we've been asked for ideas we've never tried before.'
- 'Which ideas will stretch us furthest? We'll consider practicalities later.'
- 'Which ideas would be amazing if only we can pull them off?'
- 'Which ideas would our most creative rivals be attempting right now?'
- 'Which ideas will really surprise our customers?'

Reflection

How quickly do you move to action when faced with a range of options? Do you give yourself time to be open-minded before closing a discussion down?

References

Gray, D., Brown, S. and Macanufo, J. (2010) *Gamestorming: A Playbook for Innovators, Rulebreakers and Changemakers.* O'Reilly.

Mueller, J.S., Melwani, S. and Goncalo, J.A. (2010) *The Bias Against Creativity: Why People Desire But Reject Creative Ideas.* Cornell University ILR School.

Puccio, G.J., Murdock, M.C. and Mance, M. (2005) Current developments in creative problem solving for organizations: A focus on thinking skills and styles, *The Korean Journal for Thinking and Problem Solving*, 15(2), 43–76.

1.5 Time and space

Why

You have to create time and space to use new thinking tools.

If you can't get people away from the demands of the day job, they won't relax and will only think in practical, do-able terms. When I train creative facilitators, I tell them, 'If your boss says "you've got 10 minutes, can you run a brainstorm?" you have to say no.'

The more results-driven, deadline-focused and noisy your day job is, the harder you have to work to make uninterrupted time and space for creative thinking.

Knowledge briefing

We live in an overloaded age. We hear or see up to 100,000 words a day. But we can only pay attention to around seven things at a time, according to psychologists. So we multi-task. But new research shows that switching attention from one thing to another is one of the most exhausting activities our brains can do.

Worse still, trivial decisions don't take up fewer neural resources than important ones. So deleting spam email from your inbox takes as much neural effort as finishing a report. And once you've been distracted, for example, by an email alert, it takes around 20 minutes to regain your focus on the task in hand (Hertz 2013).

What does this mean for creative thinking? Daniel Levitin identifies two modes of thought. There's a 'task positive executive network' that gets stuff done. Then there's the 'task negative network' or daydreaming mode, where you're not really controlling the direction of your thoughts. This is when the brain makes its own new connections, when new ideas and lightbulb moments come (Levitin 2014).

This is the time and space you're trying to create for new thinking. Any intrusion from the day job – emails, tweets, status updates – will push our brains back into 'task positive' mode.

How

1. Tips for creating the right space

- Get agreement from the team/boss that everyone puts on their 'out of office', no-one checks emails/tweets during the session.
- Make sure you get away from your desks, as this space is associated with the day job and our 'task positive' thinking.
- An unusual space can be stimulating, although it does need to be quiet and free from interruption.

2. Tips for creating the right time

Obvious ideas come out first, so if you only have 10 minutes, you'll only get obvious ideas. Creative thinking sessions need at least 45–60 minutes to get the best results.

- Divergent and lateral thinking tools need time to work, especially if people aren't familiar with using them.
- Convergent thinking also takes time. If you don't allow enough time for these stages, you won't have any clear next steps.
- Make a running order and stick to it (see below).

TIME	ACTION
5 MINS	INTRODUCTIONS
10 MINS	SET OUT THE CHALLENGE
30 MINS	DIVERGENT / LATERAL TOOL
10 MINS	DISCUSS AND CONVERGE
5 MINS	NEXT STEPS

Reflection

How hard do you find it to get uninterrupted time and space for new thinking? How long does it take to shake off the 'task positive' mindset?

References

Hertz, N. (2013) *Eyes Wide Open: How to Make Smart Decisions in a Confusing World.* William Collins.

Levitin, D.J. (2014) *The Organised Mind: Thinking Straight in an Age of Information Overload.* Penguin Books.

1.6 Group dynamics

Why

Ideas are born in a single mind but they live or die in groups. A good group will build on each other's ideas and bring different worldviews to bear. A bad group will kill ideas prematurely with a 'not how we do things round here' mindset.

Lots of different factors affect group dynamics: time and space (see Section 1.5 above); the size of a group; the mix of extroverts and introverts; the attitudes of senior figures in the room; the skills of the session facilitator or leader.

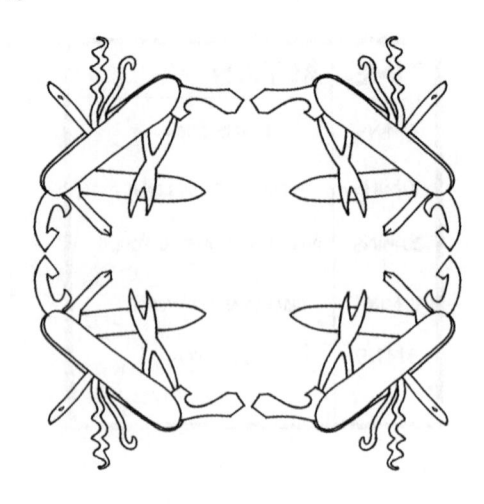

The amount of autonomy people have over how they work can have a huge influence on their willingness to take on complex creative projects.

Knowledge briefing

If you want to motivate a creative team, set a clear goal then give as much autonomy as you can. Anyone whose job involves solving difficult problems works better if they can influence the task, the hours they work, the techniques they use and the people they work with (Pink 2011). Google's head of people operations, Laszlo Bock, has a rule for autonomy: 'Give people slightly more trust, freedom and authority than you are comfortable giving them. If you're not nervous, you haven't given them enough' (Bock 2015).

People will arrive at a creative session very conscious of status and reputation. You have to give them explicit permission to behave differently – to be playful not serious. Laughter helps – it frees up the brain to make new connections (Davies 2013). Senior figures in the session have to signal very clearly that they're not there to exercise authority at this stage. Introverts need to feel that a quietly expressed idea carries as much weight as an extrovert's hasty shout (Cain 2013).

How

1. Expand your autonomy

Ask yourself and your team these questions:

How much autonomy do people actually have over different aspects of their work?	Ask people to score their own experience of autonomy. Don't assume you already know.
How much autonomy can you give people on the means to achieve any given end?	Share your goals and also share why they matter. Set parameters then offer freedom.
How can you prevent isolation if people are working more autonomously?	Good communication, shared values and workplace culture become more important if you move away from rigid office hours.
How can you measure progress if everyone is working more autonomously?	People are less likely to freeload when they know they have to account for their time at various points during a project.
Where can we test more autonomous ways of working?	Try new ways of working for 90 days with a built-in review. If it works, expand further.

2. Plan your next creative session

- *Break the ice.* Laughter removes tension, deflates egos and gets the brain making new connections, so use icebreakers (you'll find plenty online).
- *Size matters.* Splitting people into small groups helps those who won't speak up in a large group. As a rule of thumb, any group larger than four will make it hard for everyone to participate fully. But you have to allow time for small groups to feed back to the wider group (for more tips on this see Chapter 4).
- *Introverts and extroverts.* Introverts tend to hang onto an idea until it's perfect. Extroverts will say anything to fill a silence. Unless you manage this situation, one will drown out the other. Tools that involve writing and silent working help introverts contribute on an equal footing (see Section 4.3).

- *Treat ideas equally – at first.* In the divergent phase, you have to welcome all ideas – good, bad and indifferent. If you show preferences, people start trying to second-guess what you 'really' want. Just repeat 'Yes, what else?' At the end of the divergent phase, clearly signal that you've now moved on to selecting the best ideas.
- *How to handle senior leaders in a brainstorm.* How many senior leaders can act like 'one of the team'? Even if they can, how many junior staff can forget they're talking to the boss? Unless your boss is very playful and relaxed, his/her presence could stifle the free flow of tentative new ideas. Ask your senior leader to attend the first 10 minutes to set the scene – and the last 10 minutes to hear your best ideas.
- *Use a facilitator.* If *you* are the senior leader, consider using a facilitator to run it for you.
- *Keep the door open.* A well-run creative session will pump people full of ideas and stimuli. Chances are, their best ideas will pop into their heads on the way home or in the shower. Tell them to send any fresh ideas to you.

Reflection

Did the results of the autonomy audit surprise you? How would you work differently if you had greater autonomy? How did your creative session work with these new guidelines? Was it an improvement on others you've tried?

References

Bock, L. (2015) *Work Rules! Insights from Inside Google that Will Transform How You Live and Lead.* John Murray.

Cain, S. (2013) *Quiet: The Power of Introverts in a World that Won't Stop Talking.* Penguin Books.

Davies, S. (2013) *Laughology: Improve Your Life with the Science of Laughter.* Crown House Publishing.

Pink, D. (2011) *Drive: The Surprising Truth about What Motivates Us.* Canongate Books.

1.7 Choose the right tools for the job

Creative thinking is a process and it has stages. Each stage has questions you need to ask and tools that will help you move on. Neglect this and you will end up with confusion and failure, producing ideas that nobody really wants.

So, where are you now with your project? What tools do you need?

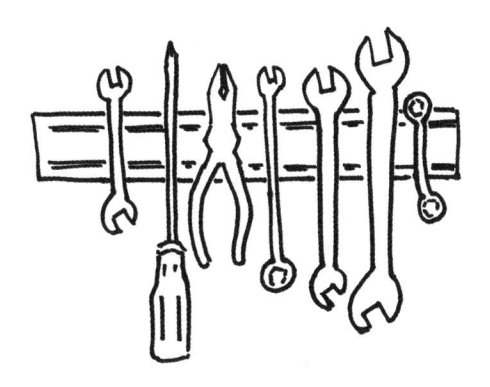

Can you answer these questions?

- *'Why are we doing this in the first place?'* If this isn't clear, make it so. Don't accept a vague or dull creative challenge from your bosses. Use the tools in Chapter 2 to keep your mission clear and exciting.
- *'Is this challenge engaging?'* If not, why not? You want people to lean in when you talk about your project, not roll their eyes. Use the tools in Chapter 3 to craft a compelling challenge that hooks people's attention.
- *'Are we really stretching ourselves to find new ideas?'* If more of the same was okay, you'd be doing it already. Use the tools in Chapter 4 to push yourself right to the edge of what's possible.
- *'Is this idea as strong as it could be?'* If you've already got a front-runner idea, don't ask people to brainstorm for more. Road-test the one you've got first. Go looking carefully for its weaknesses. The tools in Chapters 5 and 6 will help you nurture good ideas and weed out bad ones.

Be more creative

- *'How can we do better next time?'* This question is the mark of a learning organisation. Chapter 6 gives you tools to use when new ideas fail.
- *'How do I make this idea irresistible?'* It doesn't matter how good your project is if you can't get your message across to anyone else. Use tools from great storytellers and communicators in Chapter 7 to sell your idea to the people who matter most.

Chapter 2

Your creative mission

2.1 Imagine a world without you

2.2 Apply the power of why

2.3 What's your problem?

2.4 The lizard, the chimp and the business exec

2.5 Four ways of seeing

2.6 Give and take

2.7 Tweet simplicity

SPEED READ
2. Your creative mission

2.1 Imagine a world without you

Imagine a world without you. What would people miss? I don't mean you personally, I mean if the project you are working on never existed, what would we be missing out on?

IMAGINE A WORLD WITHOUT YOU

This tool creates a 'stop and think' moment. It can be the first step in working out what your creative mission is, where you're trying to go and why. It's vital to get this clear before you start, because as the American baseball player Yogi Berra once said, 'You've got to be very careful if you don't know where you are going, because you might not get there.'

In a world without your project, what would people miss? Find out what you're valued for and make that part of your mission.

Do this
Think about a person, product or service that means a lot to you. What would you miss if they didn't exist? How would you like people to think about you?

Your creative mission

2.2 Apply the power of why

Toyota's classic 'five whys' tool was designed for finding the root causes of engineers' problems. But you can also use it to get to the heart of what's motivating you or interrogate what really lies behind your challenge.

Take your mission statement and ask 'why?' Ask 'why?' again. The obvious answers will come out first. So ask 'why?' five times and see how deep you get.

> **Do this**
> Think back to a project you really loved working on. How clear was the 'why' behind what you were doing?

2.3 What's your problem?

Hitting a problem is like finding an obstacle in your way. Do nothing and you have reached a dead end. But you can borrow a tool from the world of therapy and reframe problems as open-ended questions.

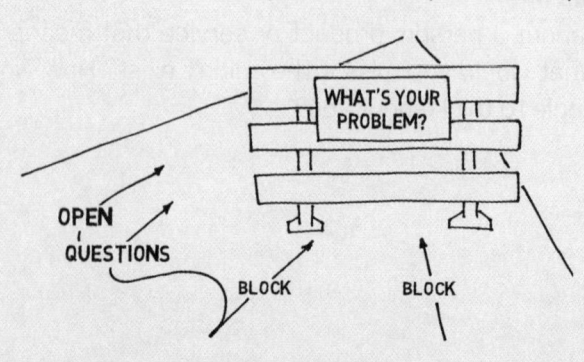

Speed read

So 'we've got no time' becomes 'how can we free up time to make this happen?'

Turning a problem into an open-ended question is like discovering that there could be ways around the obstacle. Your next challenge is to explore those ways.

Do this
Think about the biggest problem facing you. How do you feel about exploring ways around it?

2.4 The lizard, the chimp and the business exec

This bit of pop-science helps you explore where the key messages about your project land in people's minds. Our brains are shaped by our evolution. The reptilian, or lizard, part of our brain deals with fear and desire; our chimp brain deals with status and emotion; our business executive brain handles logic and reason.

LIZARD, CHIMP AND BUSINESS EXEC

You may be asked to make an argument for your project based on logic and reason. But underneath that, in the minds of the people you need to convince, there might be all kinds of hopes, fears and desires swirling around. You may need to tailor your approach to suit different audiences.

Do this
What's your biggest hope about your project? What's your biggest fear? Are they based on logical arguments or gut feelings?

2.5 Four ways of seeing

This tool, borrowed from the US military, will help you keep the people who matter at the heart of your creative mission.

FOUR WAYS OF SEEING

The 'four ways of seeing' tool teases out differences between how you see yourself and others, and compares that to how they see themselves and you. It may throw up gaps you need to close.

It's vital to check assumptions about your customers, audience or stakeholders. Misplaced assumptions lie at the heart of many failed projects.

> **Do this**
> Who are the stakeholders who really matter to the success of your project? How much do you know about them? How much do they know about you?

2.6 Give and take

If you're just starting out on a creative mission, this is a simple tool to get a project team on the same page. Working out a 'give and take' matrix allows you to map out what each person needs and see who can help others. You'll soon see any workload imbalances between givers and takers. It's also a great way to resolve any ambiguity about roles and responsibilities.

Speed read

Keep updating the matrix as your project unfolds. Display it where the team can see it – to remind them what they've promised each other.

Do this
Have you already got a sense of who's going to be a giver and who'll be a taker on your project? Is this based on experience or guesswork?

2.7 Tweet simplicity

Sum up why your project matters in 140 characters, with no jargon. A clear, compelling mission goal is your compass, signpost and yardstick.

(Note – those two sentences contain 140 characters.)

#SIMPLICITY

Your creative mission

Your mission statement needs to be clear because you'll need to repeat it over and over again as your project unfolds. It's got to be compelling so that people respond, even when they've heard it before.

Do this
Think of the projects you've worked on before. Did they have a clear mission? Did you feel it was compelling or did it become a drag?

BIG PICTURE
2. Your creative mission

2.1 Imagine a world without you

Why

Imagine the world without you. What would people miss?

IMAGINE A WORLD WITHOUT YOU

This kind of deep, existential question forces us to focus on the core of what we are doing and why.

It's hard to motivate people with nothing but a carrot-and-stick approach. Whatever level we work at, we feel more motivated if we can see the value of what we are doing in the wider world.

Knowledge briefing

This approach was used by LEGO at a dark moment in their history. Terrified by the rise of video games, LEGO launched a series of radical new ventures such as retail stores, theme parks, TV series and action figures. Costs rose and profits fell during this period of 'runaway innovation' and by 2004 LEGO stood on the brink of bankruptcy. CEO Tormod Askildsen led a senior team that asked: 'Why does LEGO exist? What would the world miss if LEGO went away?'

The answer came down to two things: the brick and the system of building. Only LEGO gave kids the flexibility to endlessly combine sets, follow instructions or build whatever they imagined. This insight helped LEGO find the core of its mission. The company rediscovered its mojo, stabilised and grew rapidly (Robertson 2013).

Google have a clear mission – to organise the world's information. This sets them apart from their competitors and gives them a focus on something other than the bottom line. It is also, as Google's head of HR points out, a never-ending mission, because the challenge keeps on growing. This allows Google to 'move forward by steering with a compass rather than a speedometer' (Bock 2015).

How

1. Imagine a world without you

- Group or solo exercise, 20 minutes.

Imagine a world without your project. Write down all the things people would miss. Think about colleagues, customers, anyone. Keep going and write as many things as you can in 10 minutes. *What makes you so special?*

Let's say your project is to improve staff development in your company by creating a new training centre. As in the example on the opposite page, you could write down all the things you would miss if you *don't* go ahead with this project. Now underline all the reasons you think matter most. What are the common themes connecting them? Can you turn these themes into your mission?

So you could turn the underlined areas into a statement:

> 'Our training programme will keep staff loyal to our company, because we're the best place to keep their technical skills fresh.'

or

> 'No-one wants to fall behind. Training keeps the company competitive and stops our individual skills going stale.'

Big picture

> **IMAGINE A WORLD WITHOUT...**
> staff training centre
> - demotivated staff
> - staff leave and work for competitors
> - rely on freelancers
> - rivals produce better products
> - can't pass on skills to new staff
> - harder to introduce new skills
> - stagnation
> - harder to improve underperformers
> - harder to reward people who want to improve
> - wasting skills of staff who could train others

2. How can you steer by compass, not speedometer?

- Group or solo exercise, 30–40 minutes. You'll need sticky notes; worksheet optional.

For this exercise:

- Draw a goal compass for each person.

```
            DESIRE
              ↑
NICE TO HAVE ←◆→ DISTRACTION
              ↓
            AVOID
GOAL COMPASS         N↑
```

Your creative mission

- Ask them to work separately, filling in a separate sticky note for all the factors your project should have as desirables, nice-to-haves, distractions or things to avoid.
- After 10 minutes, bring the group together to create one large goal compass from their individual ideas. There will be some consensus and some discussion.
- With 10 minutes to go, converge on the most important desirables, the long-term goals you should be navigating towards. (See Section 1.4 for tips on converging.)

Reflection

How does it feel to imagine life without your project? Does it strip away unimportant considerations and make you focus on the essentials?

References

Bock, L. (2015) *Work Rules! Insights from Google that Will Transform How You Live and Lead.* John Murray.

Robertson, D. (2013) *Brick by Brick: How LEGO Rewrote the Rules of Innovation and Conquered the Global Toy Industry.* Random House Business Books.

2.2 Apply the power of why

Why

The 'five whys' technique was first used in Toyota to analyse why things on their production lines failed. But you can also use it to explore why things should happen in the first place.

Wikipedia calls the 'five whys' an 'iterative question-asking technique used to explore the cause-and-effect relationships'. I call it channelling your inner four-year-old. Time to get in touch with the kid who drove your parents mad constantly asking, 'Why?'

Knowledge briefing

When you're facing tricky problems, asking 'why?' can help you restate the original problem in broader terms. This allows you to find a wider range of possible solutions (Parnes 1981).

Asking 'why?' can prevent you from solving the *wrong* problem. It can break down your original problem into a series of related problems, and one of those might offer you the best way forward. You should try to spot clusters and connections among these related problems, then rephrase the strongest ones that emerge as 'How might we . . .?' questions. 'You should spend time consciously challenging your first impression of the problem,' says author Roger Firestien. 'In fact, this is the only way you're likely to discover, then solve, the real problem' (Firestien 1996).

How

1. Use the 'five whys'

- Group exercise or solo, 30–40 minutes.

For this exercise:

- Take a large, blank sheet of paper. In the centre, write the mission statement for your project (e.g. new staff training centre). Now ask yourself 'why?' Write the answer below the statement.
- Ask 'why?' again. And again. And again. And finally, ask 'why?' again.
- By the fifth 'why?' you want to be getting into deeper emotional territory. Try to explore people's needs and values – things they feel but rarely discuss.
- Now start again. 'Why else?'

Your creative mission

> **Tip**
>
> Give this exercise a twist by throwing in variations:
>
> - Why does this matter?
> - Why do I care?
> - Why should others care?

2. Evaluate and restate

- Group exercise, 10–20 minutes.

With 10 minutes to go, look at all the reasons and pick out any insights you think are worth exploring further. Ask the group to dot vote (see Section 1.4) to choose three reasons which they think are most important.

Look for clusters and hotspots. Look for connections and common themes. Restate these as 'How could we . . .?' questions. So in the example below:

FIVE WHYS

create new staff training centre

why should staff care?

improve morale

why do I care?

I want people to do good work

staff work hard and need to feel valued

it's important to be rewarded

I want people to be happy

because work is about more than just money

it's important for me to be liked by colleagues

makes us feel good about ourselves

'How could we promote training as a non-cash benefit for staff?'

'How could we show managers that training helps them build team harmony?'

Reflection

How easy do you find it to challenge the way a problem is presented to you by repeatedly asking 'why?' How easy is it to apply to your own project, if you think you already know the answers?

References

Firestien, R. (1996) *Leading on the Creative Edge: Gaining Competitive Advantage through the Power of Creative Problem Solving.* Pinon Press.

Parnes, S. (1981) *The Magic of Your Mind.* Creative Education Foundation.

2.3 What's your problem?

Why

Think about it: when you're presented with a problem, do you start right away on the solution?

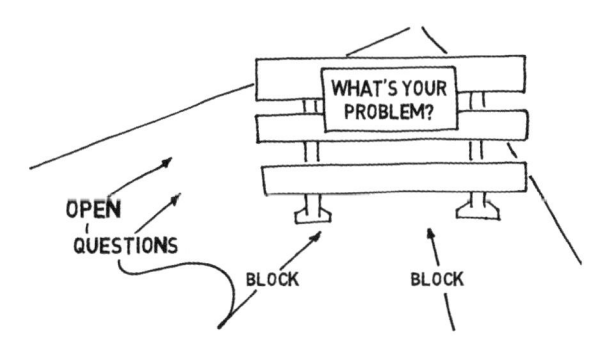

Or if it's a tough one, do you stare at it and wonder how you'll ever solve it?

How often do you challenge the problem? How often do you challenge the very language it's written in?

Knowledge briefing

'It is crucial,' according to Roger Firestien, 'to describe the problem in a way your mind considers solvable.' Of course, you won't know at first what you'll consider solvable. If you did, it wouldn't be a problem. Firestien's approach is to list all the possible ways you could restate the problem as a 'How could we . . .?' question.

If someone gives you a problem – 'we haven't got enough budget' – you can either agree or disagree. After that, you're stuck. If you reframe the same problem as an open-ended question – 'how could we find partners who bring resources to work with us?' – it provokes imagination and suggests there might be a way out. Reframing a problem into a question unblocks your mind (Firestien 1996).

Psychologist Daniel Kahneman argues that we have two thinking systems at play:

- *System 1* makes fast decisions, often based on gut instinct.
- *System 2* makes slow decisions, based on logic and reason.

Here's why we need to take a deliberate approach to reframing tough problems:

> *'Reframing is effortful and our System 2 is normally lazy. Unless there is an obvious reason to do otherwise, most of us passively accept decision problems as they are framed.'*
> (Kahneman 2011)

How

1. What's your problem?

- Group exercise or solo, 50–60 minutes.

Write your project goal in the centre of a page. Now surround it with all the problems that worry you most. Now reframe each problem as an open-ended question: 'How can we . . .?' Try to spin off at least two questions for each problem.

Let's use the training centre example again.

Big picture

WHAT'S YOUR PROBLEM?

create new staff training centre

- **staff too busy**
  - how can we run bite-sized training at lunchtimes?
  - how can we check what training staff actually want?

- **freelance trainers too expensive**
  - how can our expert staff train others?
  - how can we train with others to spread costs?

- **no senior buy-in**
  - how can we get senior staff to shape training programme?
  - how can we convince bosses?

- **not enough budget**
  - how can we convince finance department it's a good investment?
  - how can we do a cheap pilot to test?

Are there any common themes? Can you see a more solvable problem? Can you see any promising lines to follow? Can you break massive problems into bite-sized chunks and tackle them one at a time?

You might come up with answers – but even if you just get a series of good questions, you're making progress. Now decide which questions to tackle first.

Tip

If there's an elephant-in-the-room kind of problem, something everyone's thinking but no-one likes to say, now's the time to bring it out. Write it down and turn it into questions.

2. Combine 'five whys' and 'what's your problem?'[1]

- Group exercise, 40–50 minutes.

Put your notes from this exercise alongside your notes from the 'five whys'. Can you see links or common themes?

---
[1] Adapted from Firestien (1996).

Your creative mission

Try doing this as a big group exercise. Cover a whole wall in paper. Write your project mission in the middle. Write 'five whys' across one side of the paper. Then do 'what's your problem?' on the other side. Now look for common themes and links. Look for places to start work.

Reflection

Did you have a breakthrough moment when you could see a solvable problem emerging where you'd previously been stuck?

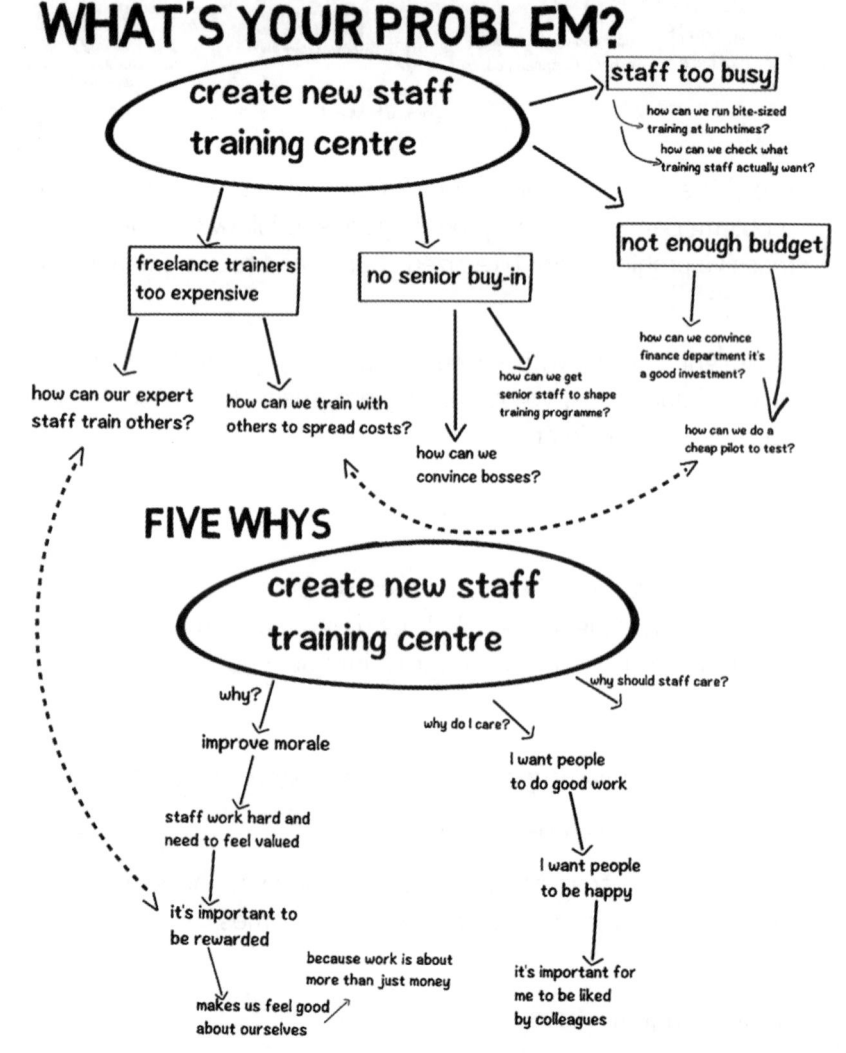

WHAT'S YOUR PROBLEM?

create new staff training centre

- staff too busy
  - how can we run bite-sized training at lunchtimes?
  - how can we check what training staff actually want?
- freelance trainers too expensive
  - how can our expert staff train others?
  - how can we train with others to spread costs?
- no senior buy-in
  - how can we get senior staff to shape training programme?
  - how can we convince bosses?
- not enough budget
  - how can we convince finance department it's a good investment?
  - how can we do a cheap pilot to test?

FIVE WHYS

create new staff training centre

- why? → improve morale
  - staff work hard and need to feel valued
  - it's important to be rewarded
  - makes us feel good about ourselves
  - because work is about more than just money
- why do I care? → I want people to do good work
- why should staff care? → I want people to be happy
  - it's important for me to be liked by colleagues

References

Firestien, R. (1996) *Leading on the Creative Edge: Gaining Competitive Advantage through the Power of Creative Problem Solving.* Pinon Press.

Kahneman, D. (2011) *Thinking, Fast and Slow.* Penguin Books.

2.4 The lizard, the chimp and the business exec

Why

Where do messages about your project land in the brains of the people you need to influence: in their lizard, chimp or business exec brain?[2]

LIZARD, CHIMP AND BUSINESS EXEC

Our lizard brain evolved first. It deals with fear and desire.

Our chimp brain is obsessed with the social glue that holds groups of primates together: emotion and status.

Our exec brain is our higher mind, the only part that can deal with logic and reason.

Appeals to the lizard brain are powerful but can provoke strong reactions. If you want to avoid negative reactions, reframe your terms (so 'fear of losing job' becomes 'desire for job security').

Strategy documents look better framed in exec terms, but can feel a bit dull. You may need to reframe your mission to suit your audience.

---

[2] Or, as they're properly known, the amygdala, cortex and neocortex. The phrase 'lizard brain' was coined in the 1960s. It's since been significantly revised (some lizards are very smart and form emotional bonds).

Knowledge briefing

An early study of human motivation divided our urges into 'base' and 'higher' drives. Abraham Maslow advanced a broad theory that we moved up a hierarchy of needs once our basic needs were satisfied.

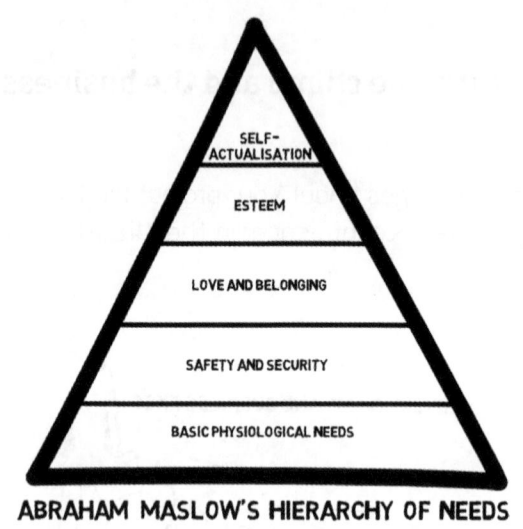

ABRAHAM MASLOW'S HIERARCHY OF NEEDS

Source: From Maslow, A.H. (1943) A theory of human motivation, *Psychology Review*, 50(4), 370–96. This content is in the public domain.

His hierarchy of five needs was reduced to just three by later researchers: existence, relatedness and growth (Kremer and Hammond 2013).

Harvard researchers Paul Lawrence and Nitin Noria suggest that we are driven to fulfil four basic needs: to acquire, bond, learn and defend. How these four needs drive our behaviour changes over time, and the different needs might contradict each other. But that's what makes human lives and choices so complex (Lawrence and Noria 2002).

How

1. The lizard, the chimp and the business exec

- Group exercise or solo, 20–30 minutes.

Big picture

Divide a piece of paper into three sections – lizard, chimp and exec. Write out your mission at the top – 140 characters or less. Write all the ways it could appeal to each part of the brain.

'How could we promote training as a benefit for staff and managers?'	
Lizard: Fear and desire	I want a better job I don't want to lose my job I'm afraid my skills are out of date
Chimp: Emotion and status	I want to be master of my craft I want others to look up to me I want to be happier in my work I want to feel less stressed I envy people with better skills than me
Exec: Logic and reason	Training leads to better motivation Training gives me transferable skills Training makes me more employable elsewhere Training is cheaper than recruitment

2. Map your project against the four needs

- Group or solo exercise, 30–40 minutes.

Write out the four headings then see how your project could appeal to those needs. Spend the first half of the session writing as many possible options as you can before converging on the strongest.

Your creative mission

'How could we promote training as a benefit for staff and managers?'	
Acquire	Earn more money ... get promoted ... find another job ... advance your career ...
Bond	Earn respect ... feel more like a part of the company ... pass on your skills to others ...
Learn	Gain mastery in your craft ... acquire new skills ... open up chances of more fulfilling work ...
Defend	Future-proof your skills ... protect yourself against redundancy ...

Source: Based on Lawrence and Noria (2002).

Reflection

Look at the results of both exercises. Do any common themes emerge? Which responses could you put at the heart of your creative mission? What makes you want to work on this project? Which themes will make your project irresistible to your customers/stakeholders?

References

Kremer, W. and Hammond, C. (2013) *Abraham Maslow and the Pyramid that Beguiled Business.* BBC World Service.

Lawrence, P.R. and Noria, N. (2002) *Driven: How Human Nature Shapes Our Choices.* Jossey-Bass.

2.5 Four ways of seeing

Why

Unchallenged assumptions can derail any project. So it's always worth checking that you and your target audience are on the same wavelength. The best way to do this is to speak to people face to face.

FOUR WAYS OF SEEING

The process of imagining how someone else sees you and your project can pay huge dividends.

Knowledge briefing

When US Army analysts picked over the mess left behind by the invasion of Iraq, they realised they'd made a fundamental error. The Allies had repeatedly promised Iraqis that things would get better after Saddam was overthrown. But as one US commander, Colonel Ralph Baker, found: 'The concept of "better" proved to be a terrible cultural misperception on our part because we, the liberators, equated better with not being ruled by a brutal dictator. In contrast, a better life for Iraqis implied consistent, reliable electricity, food, medical care, jobs, and safety from criminals and political thugs.'

Armies around the world now use Red Team analysts to test assumptions before committing to action. A common Red Team tool, the Cultural Perception Framework (aka 'four ways of seeing'), is designed to limit 'mirroring', where one side assumes the other thinks the same way as they do (University of Foreign Military and Cultural Studies 2012).

How

Cultural Perception Framework - four ways of seeing

- Group exercise or solo, 30–40 minutes.

Divide a page into four equal boxes. Then write in each box:

1. How you see yourself (your values, why you're doing the project).
2. How they (your customers/colleagues/audience) see themselves.
3. How they see you (and the project you're working on).
4. How you see them.

Your creative mission

FOUR WAYS OF SEEING

1. YOU SEE YOURSELF	2. THEY SEE THEMSELVES
- hard working - want to do high-quality work - want to help others - want this venture to succeed	- overworked - not enough time to train or develop - stressed - want to improve - too focused on the 'day job'
3. THEY SEE YOU	4. YOU SEE THEM
- care more about targets than people - not sure you're serious about training	- reluctant to engage in training - don't take advantage of existing opportunities

This example predicts reactions to setting up a new staff training programme.

Now ask yourself two questions:

1. How much of what *you* think you 'know' about *them* is fact or assumption?
2. How can you close the gap between their perception of the project and yours?

Reflection

How far can you gain insight into another group's view by imagining their reactions? How do you test your assumptions about them?

Reference

University of Foreign Military and Cultural Studies (2012) *Red Team Handbook*. UFMCS.

2.6 Give and take

Why

Have you ever been in meetings where people nod, say yes to what's being discussed ... and then do nothing?

It could be down to bloody-minded laziness or more likely 'role ambiguity'. No-one's absolutely sure who's meant to be doing what. This causes stress in the workplace, particularly when ad hoc teams come together for short projects.

You've either got to tie people down to rigid roles or find a way of getting – and keeping – them on the same page.

Knowledge briefing

Role ambiguity can be defined as 'uncertainty about the expectations, behaviors, and consequences associated with a particular role'. As long ago as 1964 it was recognised that this caused confusion, demotivation and stress, leading to high staff turnover (Kahn 1964).

But at the same time, creative projects need individuals who can tolerate ambiguity and work autonomously. Researchers say there's a balance to be struck because 'certain levels of ambiguity are necessary *in order to motivate* but beyond that, the outcomes are detrimental'. This means you may need to review roles and responsibilities several times during the life of a project (Bauer and Simmons 2000).

Your creative mission

How

1. The give and take matrix[3]

- Group exercise, 30–60 minutes.

If you have a team about to start working on your project, try this tool as a way of teasing out different needs and getting firm promises down on paper.

Let's use the example again of the project to establish a new staff training centre. You're about to sit down with:

    A: Head of HR

    B: Lead trainer in the company

    C: Head of finance (that's you)

    D: Trade union rep

Each person spends 15 minutes writing on a single, large sticky note or postcard everything they need to complete the project. This goes onto the matrix as their Take.

GIVE AND TAKE MATRIX	A.	B.	C.	D.
A.	TAKE	GIVE ↓	GIVE ↓	GIVE ↓
B.	GIVE ↑	TAKE	GIVE ↓	GIVE ↓
C.	GIVE ↑	GIVE ↑	TAKE	GIVE ↓
D.	GIVE ↑	GIVE ↑	GIVE ↑	TAKE

Source: Adapted from Gray *et al.* (2010).

---

[3] Taken from Gray *et al.* (2010).

Everyone spends five minutes reading the different Take cards. Now each person writes in the vertical columns what they can Give to help the Take.

After half an hour, you'll have a matrix of needs and promises, and you'll see any workload imbalances.

2. How ambiguous are you?

Compare your project against the four main types of role ambiguity identified by researchers (Bauer and Simmons 2000). Are you clear on all of these areas? What about the people working with you?

Type of ambiguity	Questions to ask
Goal	What is expected? What should I be doing?
Process	How should I get things done? What are the proper ways of working?
Priority	When should things be done and in what order?
Behaviour	How am I expected to act? What behaviours will lead to the needed or desired outcomes?

Source: Adapted from Bauer and Simmons (2000).

Reflection

Put the matrix up on the wall of your office during the project. Update it from time to time. Tick Gives that have been completed. Add new Takes that are needed. Just having the matrix visible in your workplace will help keep people to their promises.

Don't forget that you may need to revisit the give and take matrix so that it doesn't become a straitjacket as your project moves on.

References

Bauer, J.C. and Simmons, P.R. (2000) Role ambiguity: A review and integration of the literature, *Journal of Modern Business*, 3, 41–47.

Your creative mission

Gray, D., Brown, S. and Macanufo, J. (2010) *Gamestorming: A Playbook for Innovators, Rulebreakers and Changemakers.* O'Reilly.

Kahn, R., Wolfe, D., Quinn, R., Snoek, J. and Rosenthal, R. (1964) *Organizational Stress: Studies in Role Conflict and Ambiguity.* Wiley.

2.7 Tweet simplicity

Why

There's something wonderful about the 140-character limit forced on us by Twitter. If you can boil your mission statement down to just one tweet, in language that anyone would understand, you're doing something right.

#SIMPLICITY

So, for example, the tweet for this book in 80 characters would be: 'Tools to help you find new ideas, weed out bad ideas and sell your best ideas.' I could even add a call to action: 'Grow your own creative talents' and still come in under 140.

Note: no jargon or buzzwords – and only one word longer than six letters. Brevity forces clarity, if you work at it hard enough. If your mission statement isn't clear, perhaps it shows your thinking isn't clear either.

Knowledge briefing

You will find yourself repeating your creative mission again and again as you try to get support from different people. This is why it's important to get across a simple, big idea. 'Your audience needs to see the big picture before learning the details,' advises public-speaking coach Carmine Gallo. 'If you can't explain your idea in 140 characters, keep working at it until you can' (Gallo 2014).

Advertisers have to work with even fewer words than a tweet. Despite this, the very best adverts capture the unique proposition, or promise, behind what they're selling. The 'single-minded benefit' is at the heart of a good strategy statement, according to advertiser Pete Barry. 'Creatively speaking, it's the starting point or catalyst . . . it's the one thing the product or service stands for' (Barry 2008).

How

1. Tweet your mission

- Solo or group exercise, 10–20 minutes. You'll need pens and a stack of blank postcards.

For this exercise:

- On a postcard write out your project mission.
- Keep rewriting until you've got it down to 140 characters, no buzzwords and no jargon.
- When you've got one version, do another. Imagine you're trying to reach a different audience.

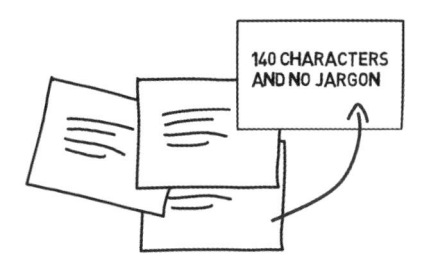

- Compare tweets. Which one grabs your attention most?
- Better still, ask your project team-mates to do the same. They might see a completely different mission than you. If this happens, don't worry – it's a wake-up call to check your assumptions. And, of course, check whether they're onto a better idea than you!

2. Think like an advertiser: what's your 'single-minded benefit'?

What is the one main benefit at the heart of your mission? What's your unique proposition?

Your creative mission

3. Signpost and yardstick

If you get this right, your mission statement can act as a signpost and a yardstick.

A clear mission statement points people in the right direction and helps them measure if they're doing the right thing along the way. When key decisions have to be made, you can ask 'Will this help us achieve the mission?' If not, why are we doing it?

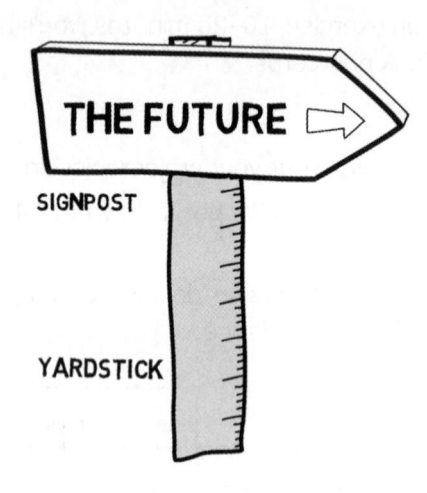

THE FUTURE ⇒

SIGNPOST

YARDSTICK

4. Check your goal compass

Go back to Section 2.1 and compare your mission statement to the goal compass. Do they fit with each other?

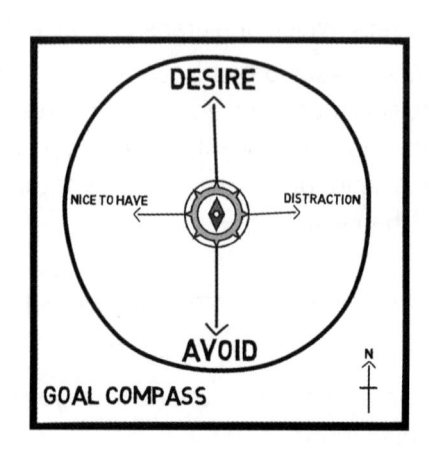

DESIRE

NICE TO HAVE ← → DISTRACTION

AVOID

GOAL COMPASS

Do they allow people to see the big picture, despite changes in the day-to-day situation? Do they allow people to navigate in the right general direction?

References

Barry, P. (2008) *The Advertising Concept Book: Think Now, Design Later.* Thames & Hudson.

Gallo, C. (2014) *Talk like TED. The 9 Public Speaking Secrets of the World's Top Minds.* Macmillan.

Chapter 3

Insights and hooks

3.1 That's funny...
3.2 Burst your filter bubble
3.3 Make connections
3.4 Use contradictions
3.5 Field trips and freshness stores
3.6 What's my motivation?
3.7 Crafting a compelling hook

SPEED READ
3. Insights and hooks

3.1 That's funny...

A good insight can make the rest of the creative process feel straightforward. But as scientist and writer Isaac Asimov said: 'The most exciting phrase to hear in science, the one that heralds new discoveries, is not "Eureka!" but "That's funny...".'

Now, it doesn't matter if it's 'funny ha ha' or 'funny peculiar'. Both are signals from the brain that something doesn't fit with the normal way of seeing the world.

'That's funny...' is the sound of your assumptions being jolted.

If you let them, those jolted assumptions itch away at the back of your brain. You can scratch that itch, challenge those assumptions and come up with brand new ideas along the way.

The rest of this chapter gives you tools to find your 'That's funny...', either from data or people.

Insights and hooks

> **Do this**
> Write down any insights you've already had about your project. Compare these to the insights you find after going through this chapter.

3.2 Burst your filter bubble

Insights can come from finding killer facts about a situation or a strong emotion that's driving people. Both have the power to turn a conversation in its tracks and force you to think again. But before we get to that stage, there's one really important thing you must do: burst your filter bubble.

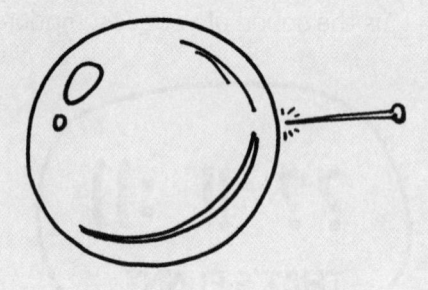

The information we get from smartphones, social media and web searches is filtered by algorithms, trying to give us more of what we want, based on what we've clicked on in the past. This filter bubble is very convenient – but also a real danger to creative thinking. It's like being surrounded by friends who only tell you what you want to hear.

You need to make deliberate efforts to diversify your data. It's about keeping an open mind for as long as possible, and that's something we often find hard.

Do this

Walk to the newsagent, go to the magazine rack and buy a publication you would never normally read: *Take A Break*, *New Statesman*, *Angling Times*, it doesn't matter. Have a good read and try to work out what assumptions and worldview its editors are working from. How are they different from yours?

3.3 Make connections

New ideas and breakthroughs can come in a flash or a slow dawning realisation. But they are often the result of connecting existing bits of information in new ways.

We must be truly open to new information and ready to spot any insights that come along. To increase the chances of spotting new connections, we have to pay attention to our networks.

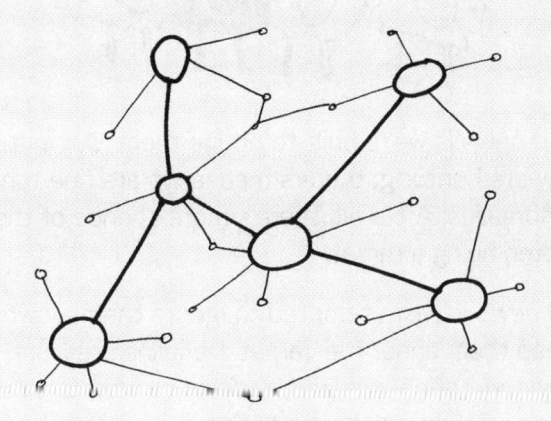

Just as ideas form inside our brains when neurons connect, so too do innovations happen in our teams when new people connect. A healthy mind needs lots of diverse stimuli and thinking time to make sense of it all. A healthy workplace needs the same – lots of diverse connections and time to take it all in.

Insights and hooks

> **Do this**
> How many new people have you connected with this week? How can you connect with one new person today?

3.4 Use contradictions

Creativity isn't just a smooth process of combining old ideas to make new ones. Sometimes there has to be a radical break with the past; old ideas have to be overthrown.

Scientific revolutions – paradigm shifts – erupt when new facts refuse to fit into old models. The old way of seeing the world has to give way and a new one emerges. Contradictions are the signs that something is refusing to fit in.

The good news is we're built to notice them. Our evolution from threat-aware hunter-gatherers means we are fine-tuned to pick up on anomalies. After all, there's more chance of the new and unexpected being a threat.

The bad news is we're tempted to ignore them, downplay them and sweep them under the carpet. Deadline pressure, tiredness, hierarchy, reputation, ego and tradition all work against us when faced with an apparent contradiction.

> **Do this**
> Quickly write down your first answer to this question:
> - How many animals of each kind did Moses take into the Ark?
> - ANSWER:

Speed read

How fine-tuned is your anomaly radar? The answer to the question is 'none', because it was Noah who took animals into the Ark, not Moses. The 'Moses Illusion' catches so many people out because they are lulled by the Biblical references to accept Moses as normal, not an anomaly. So it can be harder to spot contradictions than you first think!

3.5 Field trips and freshness stores

Great ideas rarely happen at your desk; they don't leap out at you from a screen – they come from life. When you are facing a really tough challenge, when you need to come up with bold, new ideas, then it's time to get out of the office. It's time to get face to face with that bit of the world you're trying to change. Even the best market research that money can buy is flat and two-dimensional compared with real-life experience.

Insights and hooks

You can try to take in as many facts, graphs, stories and statistics as you like about your project (in fact, you should – it's called homework!). But you will absorb knowledge of a wholly different quality and at a much deeper level if you can get out and *live* your project, even just for an afternoon. Think of it as a field trip, then make sure you spend that time with your eyes, ears and mind open.

Field trips restock your 'freshness store'. Successful creative people know that their next idea is only as good as the internal resources their brains have got to call on. These are images, concepts, facts and symbols that we all file away whenever we notice something inspiring. When you work flat-out for any period of time you start to deplete that freshness store. Your ideas start to become stale and samey.

Do this
What kind of real-world experience is closest to the project you're working on? Where could you watch people who are living with the things you are trying to change? When was the last time you saw something new just for the sake of learning or being surprised?

3.6 What's my motivation?

So far, we've talked about generating insights from killer facts – the new connections or puzzling contradictions that stick in your brain as you research your project. Another great source of insights is emotion – what motivates and drives people at a gut level.

Ask most people why they like something or behave the way they do and you won't learn much. Instead you have to play the detective, learn to ask indirect questions and tell the difference between what people say and what they mean.

The reality is most of us rarely admit what's driving us, so you have to be sensitive to small signs if you want to gain emotional insights. Happily, there are lots of tips from market researchers, focus-group leaders and even anthropologists which can help. Give them a try, because there's nothing quite like the satisfaction of gaining your own insights.

Do this
Play detective and turn the magnifying glass on yourself. How does what you say differ from what you think or how you act? How often are you explicit about your motivations?

3.7 Crafting a compelling hook

Finally, it's time to put these insights into over-drive. Killer facts and emotional drivers are useful, but you can really exploit these insights by crafting them into compelling hooks. A hook is quite simply a statement or question designed to grab someone's attention. Write a compelling hook and it will work over and over again as a starting point for new ideas.

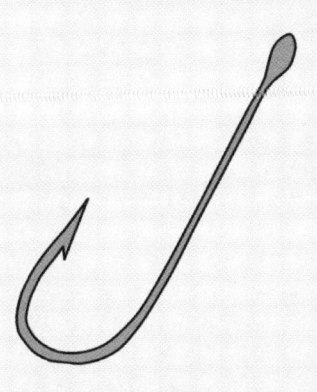

Insights and hooks

We'll use a *scriptwriting* technique to imagine what each insight could mean for different people. This lets us play out the insights with different actors, in different worlds and with different emotions at stake. Finally, we'll see how the power of *irony* – the difference between how things are and how they should be – turns the insight into an attention-grabbing hook.

> **Do this**
>
> What insights do you already have about your project? What questions do they bring to your mind? Remember, you're not trying to explain away the insight. Turning it into a compelling question will keep you coming back with new ideas.
>
> What problems have you worked on in the past which kept prompting you to find new ideas? Write down the questions you were trying to solve then. What was the compelling hook?

BIG PICTURE
3. Insights and hooks

3.1 That's funny...

Why

What's the difference between 'Eureka!' and 'That's funny...'?

Eureka!	That's funny...
Literally means, 'I have found it!'	Suggests, 'I have found *something*.'
Certain and insistent: 'This is it, we can all stop looking now.'	More humble: 'We might be onto something here, let's bear this in mind and keep looking.'

'That's funny...' is the key to finding the right questions that your project needs to answer. By the end of this chapter, you should have come up with at least one good question for your creative project.

Yes, that's right, an entire chapter to come up with a question. That might seem like overkill. But if it's the right question, if it makes people lean in and go 'ooh, that's interesting, I'd like to work on that', then it's time well spent.

Knowledge briefing

'That's funny...' is the sound of our problem-solving brain kicking in. 'Many people spend time in activities like puzzles that call for insights because the act of struggling and gaining understanding is so satisfying,' says experimental psychologist Gary Klein. 'We are built to seek insights' (Klein 2014).

Don't dismiss the importance of 'funny ha ha' either. 'Humour is the *most important* tool in your bag when it comes to playing out new thoughts,' says stand-up comedian and psychologist Stephanie

Insights and hooks

Davies. Laughter can make change seem less threatening and bind teams together. It's also an important blip on our assumption radar.

> ?? !! :))
>
> THAT'S FUNNY...

When we see or hear something that shocks us and goes against what's 'normal', our first reaction is often to laugh (Davies 2013).

Jon Rowlands cracked the problem of creating a successful show about love and relationships for young audiences who watch very little TV. His 'That's funny . . .' moment came when he watched his fiancee's stress levels rising as she planned their wedding. He stepped in to do it for her, on the assumption that it can't be that hard to plan weddings, can it? Of course, it was very hard, and

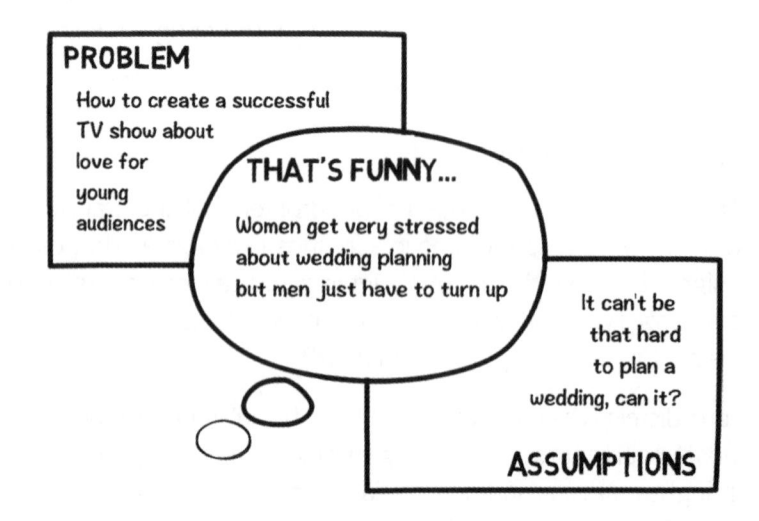

PROBLEM
How to create a successful TV show about love for young audiences

THAT'S FUNNY...
Women get very stressed about wedding planning but men just have to turn up

It can't be that hard to plan a wedding, can it?

ASSUMPTIONS

Jon turned his experience into a modern comedy of the sexes called *Don't Tell the Bride*, a BBC3 show that sold around the world (Rowlands 2015).

How

1. Find the funny

- Group or solo exercise, 20–30 minutes.

Think of a problem you or your team have solved in the past. What was your 'That's funny . . .' moment? What first struck you as odd when you looked at the situation?

```
┌─────────────────┐
│ PROBLEM         │
│         ╭───────────╮
│        ( THAT'S FUNNY... )
│         ╰───────────╯
└─────────┐  ╭──────────────┐
          ○ │              │
         ○  │   ASSUMPTIONS│
          ╰─┴──────────────┘
```

Now write down the assumptions this could be based on, including:

- yourself
- your mission
- the team
- your organisation
- your clients
- the market.

Share your list of assumptions with others on your project. Share them with people who *aren't* on your team. Do they have different assumptions? Remember, you're not trying to achieve consensus here. Different viewpoints are really valuable and conflicting assumptions are often starting points for new ideas.

Once you've identified your assumptions, you're ready to go looking for the killer facts that might build them up or overturn them. You're ready to go looking for your 'That's funny . . .'.

Reflection
When have you successfully challenged assumptions on other projects? When did you have a 'That's funny . . .' feeling about something that turned out to be important?

References
Davies, S. (2013) *Laughology: Improve Your Life with the Science of Laughter.* Crown House Publishing.
Klein, G. (2014) *Seeing What Others Don't: The Remarkable Ways We Gain Insights.* Nicholas Brealey Publishing.
Rowlands, J. (2015) *Don't Tell The Bride: The Alternative Guide to the Ultimate Wedding.* Blink Publishing.

3.2 Burst your filter bubble

Why
You've got to do your homework on your project. There's no substitute for deep understanding of the world you're operating in. This is where insights are born.

So you're doing your homework on your project. A picture starts to emerge and this becomes a framework for you to organise new information as it comes in.

Wait! Where is your information coming from? Are you inside a 'filter bubble' that's making the world seem simpler than it really is?

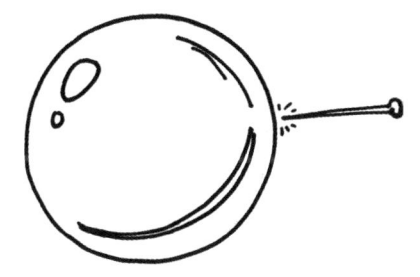

Knowledge briefing

Author and internet activist Eli Pariser described 'the filter bubble' as 'a personal ecosystem of information'. Every time you venture online, you leave a rich trail of search terms, click preferences, browsing data and cookies.

Algorithms comb through this to target you with adverts but also to send you the information they think you're *really* looking for. The implications are obvious – if you're looking for more of the same, you'll find plenty. If you are looking for surprises, for uncomfortable evidence, you'll have to try harder (Pariser 2011).

The 'filter bubble' is the latest digital version of an age-old human trait called 'confirmation bias'. Psychologist Daniel Kahneman argues that our fast-thinking, instinctive or 'gut' responses are gullible and biased towards believing things at face value. Our rational minds are in charge of doubting, but they are 'sometimes busy and often lazy'. The result is 'people seek data that are likely to be compatible with views they already hold'. It takes a deliberate effort to go looking for facts that won't fit (Kahneman 2011).

Dr Zella King, an expert on networks, suggests we should regularly review our 'go-to' sources of information to combat confirmation bias. We can diversify our sources just by deleting some of our regular news feeds and replacing them with others. Similarly, King suggests we learn more new information from 'weak ties' among our social networks – people we hardly know – than from 'strong ties' – friends and close colleagues (King 2011).

Insights and hooks

How

1. Bursting your filter bubble

- Group exercise, 30–40 minutes.

Use this diagram to map your filter bubble. Write down the trusted sources you use all the time, then the sources you're aware of but rarely use.

Now *get advice* on sources you don't know about. Which of these new sources should you bring into your bubble?

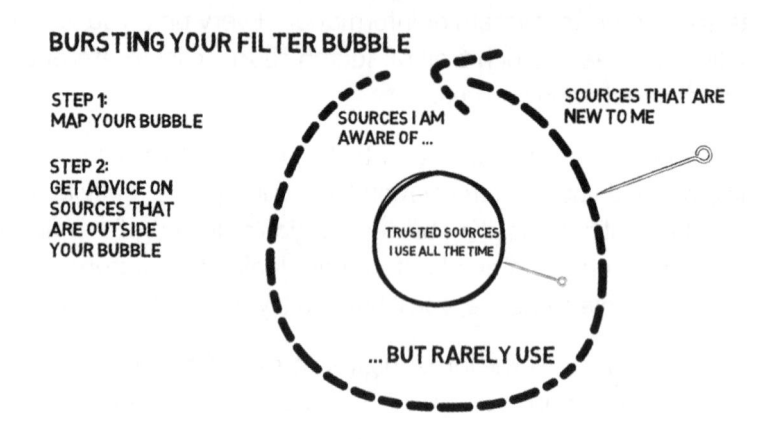

BURSTING YOUR FILTER BUBBLE

STEP 1:
MAP YOUR BUBBLE

STEP 2:
GET ADVICE ON
SOURCES THAT
ARE OUTSIDE
YOUR BUBBLE

SOURCES I AM AWARE OF ...

SOURCES THAT ARE NEW TO ME

TRUSTED SOURCES I USE ALL THE TIME

... BUT RARELY USE

- Compare bubbles with the rest of your team.
- Beware of over-reliance on the same trusted sources.
- Get advice from outside the team on sources that are new to all of you.
- Which of these new sources should you bring into your team's bubble?

Big picture

BURSTING YOUR FILTER BUBBLE

STEP 3:
COMPARE BUBBLES WITH OTHERS IN YOUR TEAM

STEP 4:
BEWARE OF OVER-RELIANCE ON THE SAME TRUSTED SOURCES

STEP 5:
GET ADVICE FROM OUTSIDE THE TEAM ON SOURCES THAT ARE NEW TO YOU ALL

- SOURCES WE ARE AWARE OF...
- SOURCES THAT ARE NEW TO OUR TEAM
- TRUSTED SOURCES
- ...BUT RARELY USE

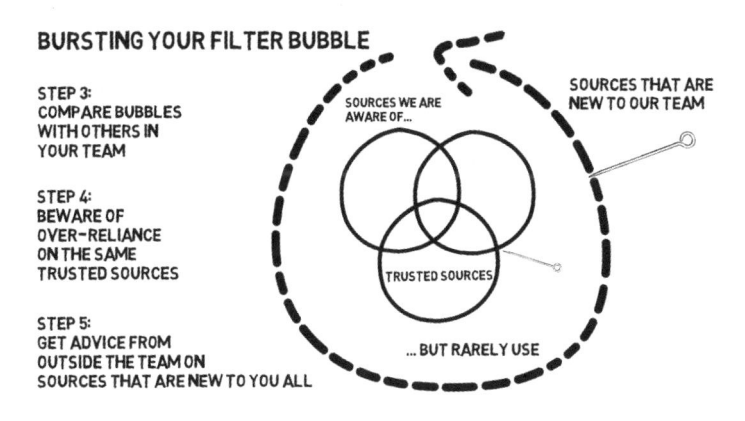

2. Diversify your sources of data

Try these habits over the next few weeks.

- Pick up a newspaper or magazine you normally avoid. What is the difference between its worldview and yours?
- Try replacing some of your 'go-to' sources of information. So if you follow *New Scientist* on Twitter, replace it for a few weeks with *Scientific American*.
- Exploit your weak ties. Don't just read comments and blogs from close colleagues and friends. Look instead to the wider reaches of your network.
- Reduce the influence of algorithms. Set up a separate browser where you constantly delete search history – or use a search engine that deliberately doesn't track you.
- Find good curators who assess lots of different viewpoints, rather than promoting one. Just make sure your curators don't all share the same viewpoint.

Reflection

Where has surprising new data come from on previous projects you've worked on? How did you react to it? How do you react now to data from unusual sources?

References

Kahneman, D. (2011) *Thinking, Fast and Slow*. Penguin Books.
King, Z. (2011) *Who Is in Your Camp?* The Social Life of Ideas blog: http://sociallifeofideas.blogspot.co.uk/2011/11/who-is-in-your-camp.html
Pariser, E. (2011) *The Filter Bubble: What the Internet Is Hiding from You*. Penguin Books.

3.3 Make connections

Why

Apple's co-founder Steve Jobs famously said that 'creativity is just connecting things'. The trick, Jobs said, is to make sure you accumulate enough diverse experiences in your life to connect in new and surprising ways.

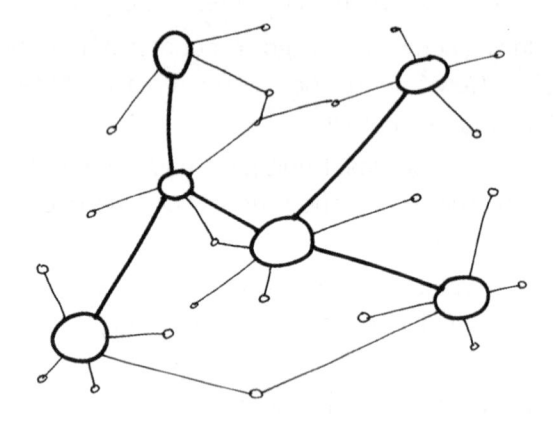

There are countless examples of inventions and breakthroughs which have come from connecting things. Gutenberg adapted wooden grape presses from the wine industry to make the world's first printing press. Sir Tim Berners-Lee was inspired by the encyclopaedia he read as a child when developing the World Wide Web. Even The Beatles started life as a covers band, learning from Buddy Holly, Little Richard and Elvis before striking out on their own.

Knowledge briefing

'Combinatorial creativity' is widely studied, both at the individual and organisational levels. Mihaly Csikszentmihalyi interviewed 91 exceptional thinkers – scientists, writers, artists – and found again and again that 'most creative achievements depend on making connections among disparate domains'. Csikszentmihalyi says we should be interested in a wide range of things for their own sake, and that the geniuses he met retained childlike curiosity long into old age (Csikszentmihalyi 1996).

In his study of 'the natural history of innovation', author Steven Johnson says ideas fade slowly into view, building up over time as 'slow hunches'. All kinds of networks, from internet groups to chats in the works canteen, allow more of these hunches to connect. If you want more new ideas, make it easier for slow hunches to collide. When it comes to innovation, Johnson says, 'chance favours the connected mind' (Johnson 2010).

Organisational cultures can inhibit connections. At Pixar, founder Ed Catmull realised that animators weren't 'allowed' to discuss ideas with technicians without going through line managers first. Catmull created an explicit new rule: 'Anyone should be able to talk to anyone else, at any level, at any time, without fear of reprimand.' Getting information to flow freely was more important to Pixar's survival than protecting managers' egos (Catmull and Wallace 2014).

How

1. How can you make it easier for 'slow hunches' to connect in your team or workplace? Stop eating lunch at your desk and go to the canteen. Have an unexpected conversation and give your brain some vital breathing space.
2. Can you open your creative process up to as many people as possible, never mind what formal role they play in the organisation? (See Chapters 4 and 5 for tools to make this easier.)

3. Organise a 'speed date' in your workplace. On each rotation, ask three questions: What are you passionate about? What are you working on right now? How could I help?
4. Do you need permission to speak? Can you introduce the Pixar rule, if not in your entire organisation then at least in your team?

Reflection

How many people know what their colleagues are passionate about – inside and outside work? How could you use blogs, posters, short films or networking events to make people feel more connected?

References

Catmull, E. and Wallace, A. (2014) *Creativity, Inc. Overcoming the Unseen Forces that Stand in the Way of True Inspiration.* Bantam Press.

Csikszentmihalyi, M. (1996) *Creativity: The Psychology of Discovery and Invention.* HarperCollins.

Johnson, S. (2010) *Where Good Ideas Come From: The Natural History of Innovation.* Penguin Books.

3.4 Use contradictions

Why

When Galileo Galilei observed the heavens through a telescope, he saw planets moving in a way that didn't make sense if you assumed the Earth was the centre of the universe. Unfortunately for Galileo, pretty much everyone *did* assume that – including the Catholic Inquisition. He was tried as a heretic and forced to recant. But the orbit of planets was an observable fact that contradicted existing theories. Eventually, the only way to resolve these contradictions was to re-order the solar system and accept that the Earth goes round the sun.

Creativity can be a messy process with plenty of conflict over ideas and between people. Contradictions can be the flashpoints in those conflicts – places where disagreement becomes unavoidable. Contradictions suggest mistakes and that can be unsettling: if we're doing the right thing, how come this doesn't fit?

This is why workplace cultures emerge in which it's hard to challenge the orthodoxy. This may help reduce error or uncertainty. But it can mean you're missing clues to something new.

Knowledge briefing

Contradictions arise from anomalies or problematic assumptions, and they set off an alarm bell in our brains. 'Contradictions signal that there's something significantly wrong with the story we're currently telling ourselves,' according to psychologist Gary Klein (Klein 2014). We are hardwired to detect anything that deviates from our definition of 'normal'. It takes two-tenths of a second for your brain to react to the anomaly in this sentence: 'Earth revolves around the trouble every year' (Kahneman 2011).

'Creative people are constantly surprised,' says Mihaly Csikszentmihalyi in his study of creative genius. 'They don't assume that they understand what is happening around them, and they don't assume that anybody else does either' (Csikszentmihalyi 1996).

Insights and hooks

How

1. Turn contradictions into insights

- Group or solo exercises, 30–40 minutes.

When our understanding of the world is suddenly thrown by a contradiction, we can pretend it hasn't happened or we can exploit it in one of two ways:

- Find and replace the weak assumption behind the contradiction with a better one.
- Rewrite the current theory or explanation.

Either way, we have created a better story to explain the world.

Case study

Prairie fires - find and replace the weak assumption

Nineteenth-century American settlers learned to limit the spread of prairie fires by setting smaller, controlled 'back-fires' in their path. Back-fires burned up the available fuel before the main fire struck. The common-sense assumption – 'never start fires on a tinder-dry prairie' – had to be replaced with a better one – 'fight fire with fire' – when the need arose.

Case study

Cholera outbreaks - rewrite current theory

Victorian doctors believed cholera was spread by breathing in foul air. But physician John Snow realised cholera victims had damage to their digestive tracts but their *lungs were intact*. This didn't fit the airborne germ theory. Snow's research eventually identified polluted water supplies as the real culprit.

Big picture

Let's try the example project from earlier in the book: improving workplace training schemes. Assume the contradiction is that everyone says they *want* training, but uptake is low. The current theory says that staff are just too busy.

CONTRADICTIONS

OPTION 1: REWRITE CURRENT THEORY/EXPLANATION

OPTION 1: REWRITE CURRENT THEORY/EXPLANATION

1. **WHAT DOESN'T FIT** — People say they want training but uptake is low

2. **CURRENT THEORY** — Staff are too busy

---

3. **WRITE LOTS OF POSSIBLE ALTERNATIVE THEORIES OR EXPLANATIONS**

   We're offering the wrong kind of training

   People don't care about career progression in this company

   People don't think our qualifications are worthwhile

   Formal training isn't the best way to improve

   Managers won't release people to be trained

   Managers don't value staff development

4. **TAKE EACH ALTERNATIVE THEORY. ASK YOURSELF 'IF THIS WAS TRUE, WHAT WOULD WE EXPECT TO SEE?'**

   Staff requesting training we don't offer

   People leaving to join companies they care more about

   People studying for qualifications outside work

   Managers struggling to fill skills gaps

   Complaints about lack of training

Insights and hooks

CONTRADICTIONS

> **5. HAVE YOU SEEN ANY EVIDENCE TO SUPPORT ALTERNATIVE THEORIES? HOW COULD YOU INVESTIGATE FURTHER?**
>
> Do we record requests for training we don't offer?
>
> How can we find out what people study outside work?
>
> How can we encourage informal learning at work?

Let's try it with the same example, but this time replacing weak assumptions:

CONTRADICTIONS

> **OPTION 2: FIND AND REPLACE WEAK ASSUMPTIONS**
>
> **1. WHAT DOESN'T FIT**   People say they want training but uptake is low
>
> **2. LIST CURRENT ASSUMPTIONS**
>
> - [x] Staff need training to develop careers
> - [ ] Our training meets their needs and industry standards
> - [ ] We have fixed budget for staff training
> - [ ] We know what our skills gaps are
> - [x] We know what skills we need in 18 months' time
> - [ ] We use training to reward and retain staff
> - [x] Training fosters loyalty to the company
> - [x] **TICK ANY ASSUMPTIONS THAT YOU FIND WEAK, CONFUSING OR UNCOMFORTABLE**

> **3. WHAT ARE THE ALTERNATIVES TO THESE ASSUMPTIONS?**
>
> Staff prefer to be trained outside our company
>
> Staff might have a better idea what skills they need in 18 months' time
>
> Training makes people more valuable and more likely to leave for a better job
>
> **4. HOW CAN YOU TEST THESE NEW ASSUMPTIONS? WHAT ADVANTAGES COULD THEY BRING?**
>
> Could we 'pool' training plans with other companies?
>
> Could we get senior staff to train junior staff?
>
> How do we reward this?
>
> How can staff who are leaving pass on their knowledge?

Reflection

When have you come up with a better story for explaining a situation? How did contradictions help you?

References

Csikszentmihalyi, M. (1996) *Creativity: The Psychology of Discovery and Invention.* HarperCollins.
Kahneman, D. (2011) *Thinking, Fast and Slow.* Penguin Books.
Klein, G. (2014) *Seeing What Others Don't: The Remarkable Ways We Gain Insights.* Nicholas Brealey Publishing.

3.5 Field trips and freshness stores

Why

If you've ever had to put up with a team 'away-day', maybe this question has crossed your mind. Why do people relocate their colleagues to a dull, corporate hotel, equip them with all the trappings of a dull office (flip charts, presentations, meeting rooms) and then expect fresh, new ideas to emerge?

If you really want to provoke fresh thinking, don't replace one boring space with another. There are two kinds of out-of-office trip to consider:

1. Field trips: going somewhere that's directly related to your project, spending time with the people who you're trying to reach.
2. Unrelated field trips: going somewhere which has nothing to do with the immediate task in hand, but is so interesting it will restock your 'freshness store' of ideas.

Knowledge briefing

The Pixar animators who made *Ratatouille* visited Parisian kitchens. The *Monsters Inc.* team hung out in Harvard student dorms. Animators on *Finding Nemo* learned to scuba dive. Pixar believe that field research is the best way to avoid derivative, uninspiring work (Catmull and Wallace 2014).

'Nothing beats getting out of the office and being with the people for whom all the work is designed,' argues business writer

Margaret Heffernan. 'Great ideas don't come from offices, but from life' (Heffernan 2015).

Watching how people interact with a product or service in their 'real world' is a much richer experience than reading market research reports. Real settings are full of triggers and cues that could help you see your project in a wider context, explore misconceptions or identify unmet needs (Bystedt *et al.* 2003).

But the second kind of trip – unrelated but fascinating – can be even more rewarding. These trips restock the 'freshness store' of images and ideas inside our heads (Allan *et al.* 2002). George Lois, a veteran US ad-man, insists on a weekly trip to a museum or art gallery. 'Nothing comes from nothing, you must continuously feed the inner beast that sparks and inspires,' he writes (Lois 2012).

Our subconscious mind throws up solutions to problems almost without trying, combining from an almost infinite number of memories, thoughts and fragments stored in our brains. 'Other things being equal,' W.I.B. Beveridge wrote, 'the greater our store of knowledge, the more likely it is that significant combinations will be thrown up' (Beveridge 1957).

We can gain new insights from curated collections of ancient wisdom – found in museums and art galleries. Objects or actions which survive for generations 'must be good at serving some hidden purpose that only time can see', according to philosopher Nassim Nicholas Taleb. 'They correspond to something deep in our nature' (Taleb 2012).

How

1. Take a field trip

- Group or solo exercise, needs at least half a day. You'll need a notebook, pen and camera or camera-phone.

1. *Plan a field trip like Pixar.* Where can you go that is closest to the project you are working on? Who are you ultimately trying to engage with and where will you find them? Plan this trip as early as you can in your creative process.

Insights and hooks

2. *People-watch like an anthropologist.* Make notes of anything people say and do that grabs your attention. Sketch out a map of where people rush, gather or linger. See if you can identify *subgroups* and *stars* in the crowd (stars are influential figures in a subgroup). Imagine what's shaping their behaviour, or better still, ask (but read Section 3.6 first).
3. *Be present (switch off your distractions).* There's no point taking yourself out of the office if you let the office come with you, in the form of a constantly pinging mobile phone. Set your out-of-office reply, put your phone on silent. Focus on what's right in front of you – things and people – not what's in your inbox or news feed.
4. *Appreciate the shock of the old.* Get up close to really old objects in a museum. Ask yourself these questions:
   - How is it used?
   - What hidden purpose could it have?
   - Who owns it, who shares it?
   - How is it adapted? What else is it used for?
   - How does it make us feel?
   - Does it have a symbolic or ritual significance?
   - How does it correspond to something deep in our nature?
   - How can you apply these insights to your creative challenge?

(Try the *Shock of the Old* photocards at www.newthinking.tools/downloads.)

> **Tip**
>
> What if you can't spend time on a field trip into your project world?
>
> - *Use your local newsagent.* There are roughly 8,000 magazine titles published in the UK each year. So if you're working on a new product or service for budget-conscious young mums,

> for example, buy the magazines they're buying – *Take a Break, Hello, Heat, Closer, Chat* and *OK!*.[4]
>
> - *These magazines spend years getting to know their audiences.* A successful magazine is a peek into the soul of its readers. Every page – even adverts – can tell you something about them and how they see the world.

Reflection

Try a mini version of a field trip on your morning commute – or in the workplace canteen. What can you observe about your fellow commuters or colleagues? What would an outsider see?

Keep a notebook handy, use a note-taking app on your phone or even just your smartphone's camera. Every time you come across something that grabs your attention for any reason, make a note or snap a picture.

Why not get an old-fashioned pin-board up in your workspace? Photos, articles, notes or doodles on a wall might spark new thoughts when you least expect it.

References

Allan, D., Kingdon, M., Murrin, K. and Rudkin, D. (2002) *Sticky Wisdom: How to Start a Creative Revolution at Work*. ?WhatIf! Publications.

Beveridge, W.I.B. (1957) *The Art of Scientific Investigation*. W.W. Norton & Co.

Bystedt, J., Lynn, S. and Potts, D. (2003) *Moderating to the Max: A Full Tilt Guide to Creative, Insightful Focus Groups and Depth Interviews*. Paramount Market Publishing.

Catmull, E. and Wallace, A. (2014) *Creativity, Inc. Overcoming the Unseen Forces that Stand in the Way of True Inspiration*. Bantam Press.

---

[4] These six titles sell to six million C2DE women every week, according to the magazine industry's *National Readership Survey*.

Insights and hooks

Heffernan, M. (2015) *Beyond Measure: The Small Impact of Big Changes*. TED Audio Books.

Lois, G. (2012) *Damn Good Advice (For People with Talent): How to Unleash Your Creative Potential by America's Master Communicator*. Phaidon Press.

Taleb, N.N. (2012) *Antifragile: Things that Gain from Disorder*. Penguin Books.

3.6 What's my motivation?

Why

Truly useful insights come from people, not screens. They are lurking in what people say, what they do and the subtle differences in between.

Market researchers, detectives and novelists find vital clues by listening carefully to what we say – and trying to work out what we're not saying.

If your project ultimately has to connect with people – customers, decision-makers, users – then spend some time with those people, pick up clues from their lives.

Even if you work in a company with a market research department, it is still worth doing this. Our brains take in 100,000 fragments of sensory data at any one time from our surroundings. No market research document could hope to capture a fraction of this input. But your brain will absorb this richness any time you walk into a new setting – and you never know what fresh nugget of information it will throw back at you when you need it most.

Knowledge briefing

We go through life mostly unaware of the sources of our own preferences, prejudices or attitudes. Market researchers say that what *we think we know* isn't fixed but needs to be reconstructed in the moment of telling. 'Laddering' techniques, where questions progress from features and attributes to benefits and finally to values, can tease out what really motivates people. Speaking to people in their 'natural' surroundings allows them to *show* you as well as *tell* you what they mean (Bystedt et al. 2003).

In fact, the obvious question 'Why?' may not help us understand other people's behaviour. 'Direct questioning ... could draw a blank or invoke an answer which is *thought to be acceptable*,' according to experienced interviewer Paul Hague. If you put people on the spot, they will often say what they think you want to hear. Indirect or 'projective' questions, using symbols, analogies, word associations, role play and even cartoons can get to the heart of what people are really thinking (Hague 1995).

How

1. Getting away from direct 'why?' questions when seeking insights from others

Let's use the example again of a project to improve training in the workplace.

- *Indirect:* 'What do you think people in your position would say about current training provision?'
- *Analogy:* 'If our workplace training was like a car, what type would it be?'
- *Word association:* 'What words would you associate with the perfect training scheme?'

Insights and hooks

- *Future scenario:* 'In two years' time, what could our training look like?'
- *Role play:* 'If you were in charge of the budget, what would your priorities be?'

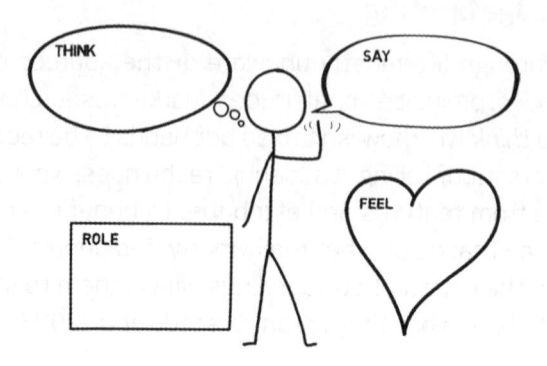

- *Cartoon:* 'Write down what trainees say, think and feel about our training programme. Now do the same for HR managers etc.'
- *Follow-up questions:* go deeper into the picture people are painting for you. Would the car be fast or reliable? What other words would you associate with a perfect training scheme? At this stage, it's okay to ask some 'why?' questions, such as 'why do you think people feel that way?'

2. Show and tell

Here's one trick I learned as a TV reporter – if you want to get authentic sound-bites, interview people as they are *doing* the thing they are talking about. Only interview them at a desk or in a studio as a last resort. It is always better to *show AND tell*. As soon as we engage our hands or bodies in activity, what comes out of our mouths is more natural.

3. Build a ladder

- Group or solo exercise, 40–60 minutes.

Start asking questions at the bottom of the ladder and slowly work up. You should expect to find more attributes, fewer benefits and just a few values at the top.

Big picture

DECISION-MAKING LADDER

VALUES — WHY ARE THESE BENEFITS IMPORTANT TO YOU? HOW DO THEY MAKE YOU FEEL? WHAT DOES THIS SAY ABOUT YOUR VALUES?

BENEFITS — WHAT BENEFITS DO THESE ATTRIBUTES BRING? WHAT WOULD YOU MISS IF THEY WEREN'T THERE? HAS THIS CHANGED OVER TIME?

ATTRIBUTES — WHAT DO YOU LIKE ABOUT ...? WHAT DO YOU WANT FROM ...? WHAT'S MOST IMPORTANT ABOUT ...?

WORK YOUR WAY UP THE LADDER

Source: Based on Bystedt *et al.* (2003).

Do several of these laddering exercises with different people and then compare results. Do common motivations emerge?

4. Make good field notes

- Jot down anything that grabs your attention, or take lots of photos on your phone.
- Write up your thoughts as soon as you can after your trip.
- Make a collage of photos, phrases and ideas and stick it on your workplace wall.

Reflection

Allow time for the observations you've made to swirl around in your mind. The day after your field trip, look back at the notes and photographs. See if any new motivations occur to you now.

References

Bystedt, J., Lynn, S. and Potts, D. (2003) *Moderating to the Max: A Full Tilt Guide to Creative, Insightful Focus Groups and Depth Interviews.* Paramount Market Publishing.

Hague, P. (1995) *Interviewing: The Market Research Series.* Kogan Page.

Insights and hooks

3.7 Crafting a compelling hook

Why

Blake Snyder was a top Hollywood scriptwriter and author of a brilliant book on how to write a movie. After a career spent in Tinseltown, what Snyder (2005) didn't know about hooking people's attention wasn't worth knowing. Snyder reckoned *irony* wins every time.

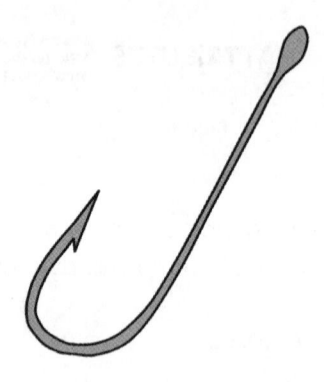

'A cop comes to L.A. to visit his estranged wife and her office building is taken over by terrorists. A businessman falls in love with a hooker he hires to be his date for the weekend . . . Both of these pitches (*Die Hard* and *Pretty Woman*) . . . fairly reek of irony,' he wrote. 'And irony gets my attention . . . it's emotionally intriguing, like an itch you have to scratch.'

Irony can help us turn a killer fact or emotional insight into a compelling hook. This is a brilliant way to turbo-charge the creative process. A compelling hook will keep you coming back again and again with more new ideas.

Knowledge briefing

Irony is the difference between how things should be and how they really are. It is not the same as sarcasm (using irony to mock) or hypocrisy (claiming more virtue than your actions suggest). If in doubt, think of Channel 4's hit comedy *Father Ted* or Chaucer's

Big picture

Canterbury Tales – priests are meant to be humble, pious and virtuous, not drunken, lazy and greedy.

For the ancient Greeks, irony was a dramatic device where the audience were in on the joke before the actor – which explains why someone writing 'Your so stupid!' is so deliciously ironic.

How

So far, so amusing – but how does it help you with your creative project? Back to Hollywood for a moment. Which film would you rather go and see:

> *Man saves island community by hunting down a giant killer shark.*

or

> *New York cop who is terrified of water saves the island community he loves by hunting down a giant killer shark in a tiny boat.*

Both pitches for *Jaws* have *actors* and a *world* in which the action takes place. Inject some *irony* – tough cop Chief Brody is *afraid of water* – and you've got our attention. Then raise the *emotional stakes* too – fear, love, hate and so on. We're hardwired to respond to these stimuli.

Let's try this on an insight I came across in a business article:

> *75% of us don't know, when asked at 4pm today, what we're having for our evening meal tonight.*[5]

1. Actor, world, emotion and irony

- Group or solo exercise, 20–30 minutes. You'll need sticky notes; worksheet optional.

---

[5] Supermarkets are 20 years out of date, says Waitrose boss, *Daily Telegraph*, 22 October 2014: http://www.telegraph.co.uk/finance/newsbysector/epic/tsco/11178281/Supermarkets-are-20-years-out-of-date-says-Waitrose-boss.html

99

Insights and hooks

For this exercise:

- List lots of possible *actors*, each on a separate sticky note: these could be budget-conscious shoppers, working parents, teenagers, takeaway owners...
- List lots of different *worlds*: in the office, on the bus, rush-hour traffic, corner shop, supermarket etc.
- Now *emotions*: desire to feed family, we want to be healthy, food is pleasurable...
- Finally *irony*: good food takes time, but we're all in a rush; we love TV chefs but never actually cook their recipes; we work hard for our family's sake, but that means we're too tired to make family meals...

COMPELLING HOOK

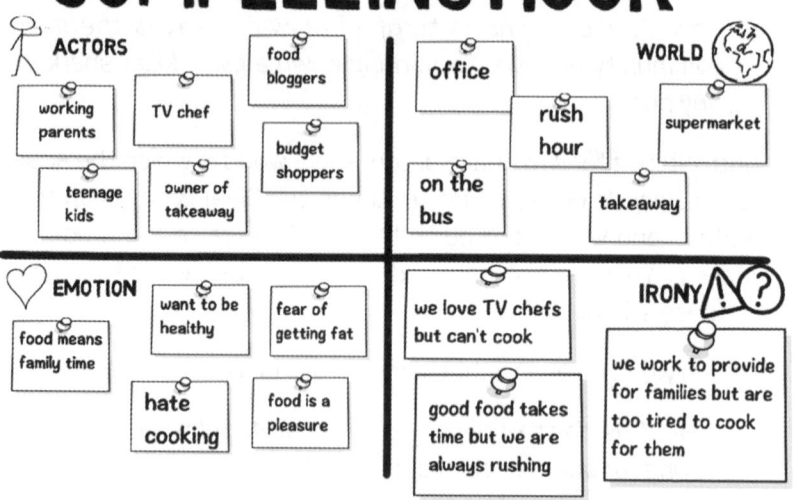

ACTORS: working parents, TV chef, food bloggers, budget shoppers, teenage kids, owner of takeaway

WORLD: office, rush hour, supermarket, on the bus, takeaway

EMOTION: food means family time, want to be healthy, fear of getting fat, hate cooking, food is a pleasure

IRONY: we love TV chefs but can't cook, good food takes time but we are always rushing, we work to provide for families but are too tired to cook for them

Try different combinations of actor, world, emotion and irony. Arrange these on the worksheet to make sentences that go: 'How could... because... despite...'

Big picture

COMPELLING HOOK

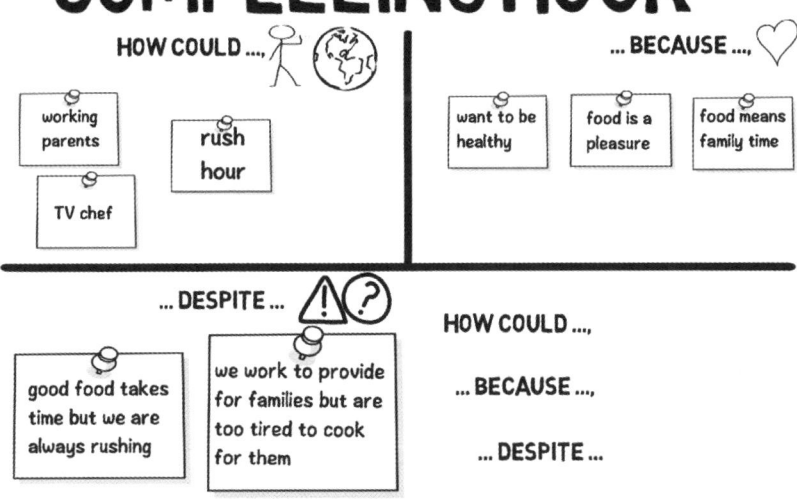

HOW COULD ...,

- working parents
- rush hour
- TV chef

... BECAUSE ...,

- want to be healthy
- food is a pleasure
- food means family time

... DESPITE ...

- good food takes time but we are always rushing
- we work to provide for families but are too tired to cook for them

HOW COULD ...,

... BECAUSE ...,

... DESPITE ...

These will be long-winded at first:

> 'How could a TV chef's food blog help hardworking parents caught up in the commute home plan a pleasurable meal, because that makes family mealtime special, despite the fact we're normally too tired to cook the kind of family meal we'd like to, even though we love our families?'

Now boil it down to something a bit snappier:

> 'How could a food blog help hardworking parents become Rush Hour Gourmets?'

Rush Hour Gourmet – actor, world and irony all contained in three little words.

2. Now have a go with your project

- Group or solo exercise, 30–40 minutes.

List your:

- 'That's funny . . .' insights (3.1)
- Surprising data from outside your filter bubble (3.2)

Insights and hooks

- Interesting connections (3.3)
- Troublesome contradictions (3.4)
- Field trip insights (3.5)
- Emotional motivators (3.6)

Write down all the possible actors, worlds, emotions and ironies you can think of. Mix and match to get different questions. What hooks your interest?

Reflection

When you think you've got a compelling hook for your project, try it out on friends and colleagues. Try using it as the title of an email or blog post – and see if you get more reaction than normal.

Reference

Snyder, B. (2005) *Save the Cat: The Only Book on Scriptwriting that You'll Ever Need.* Michael Wiese Productions.

Chapter 4

Forced inspiration

4.1 Brainstorm rules

4.2 The lateral nudge and metaphor mash

4.3 Mapping your thoughts

4.4 Steal from the heart

4.5 Break the rules

4.6 Look harder inside the box

4.7 Brainwriting tools

SPEED READ
4. Forced inspiration

4.1 Brainstorm rules

When do you have your best ideas? In the shower, driving to work, walking the dog or just staring out of the window? For me, it's on my bike. Relax, stop concentrating, or do something you love, and ideas just seem to flow.

But what if you need a whole team to come up with new ideas, to a deadline? You can't get everyone to stare out of the window together.

This is why we brainstorm. Think of it as forced inspiration.

If you don't get the rules of the game right, no-one will play nicely. You won't get the new ideas you need. Worse still, you might actually stop smart individuals coming up with their own ideas and enforce tepid groupthink.

Academics have pointed out why some brainstorms fail. The techniques and rules in this chapter have been designed to combat the main weaknesses.

Forced inspiration

> **Do this**
> Think about the last brainstorm you went to. Did you get good ideas or was it a waste of time? Did anyone explain the rules before you started?

4.2 The lateral nudge and metaphor mash

These techniques make people use images or symbols rather than words as their starting point or inspiration. Use the lateral nudge towards the end of an ideas session. By then, all the obvious ideas will have come out.

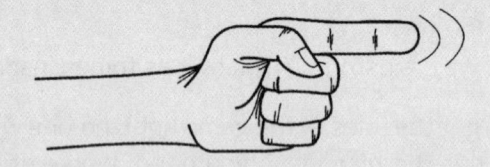

People might be feeling like the job's done and they can stop. They'll be surprised how many new ideas they've got left in them, and just how original they can be. Or you can devote a longer session to the metaphor mash – a beefed up version of the lateral nudge. It takes longer to use but really stretches you and your team.

We love finding meaning and symbolism all around us, and both of these tools exploit that common urge. Starting your creative thinking in images rather than words feels strange at first. But the harder people have to work to find an idea, the more excited they get when it comes. You will surprise yourselves with the range of ideas you can get from throwing a random set of images together.

> **Do this**
> Stare out of the window next time you've got a spare moment. What can you see? How many different things could it symbolise?

4.3 Mapping your thoughts

These techniques take doodling and scribbling around the margins of an idea to a whole new level. Like other creative techniques, this involves a divergent thinking approach – encouraging you to surround your original proposition or idea with as many linked options as you can.

Mapping techniques are very flexible: you can use them on your own or in large groups. You can link ideas by how they directly relate (a concept map) or by looser associations (a mind map). You can create several maps and bring them together on one super-map.

Mapping can be time-consuming when done properly, but the results – a giant road-map of all your important ideas – can go up on the wall in your workspace and provide inspiration for you long after the brainstorm.

There are all kinds of mapping apps and software available for computer or tablet, making it easier to create maps by yourself to share online.

> **Do this**
> Try a web search for free mind-mapping tools available online.

4.4 Steal from the heart

We're all inspired by other people's work, so much so that we inevitably copy. If we slavishly copy one source (and try to hide our tracks), it's plagiarism. If we use several sources, adapting as we go along, that's inspiration. These tools formalise the magpie-like stealing that goes on in our heads all the time.

First, you work out what's at the heart of your project. Then ask yourself who else is brilliant at achieving similar ends and how you can adapt some of that brilliance to meet your needs. Alternatively, you can set out an array of different qualities from the things that inspire you and force new combinations.

These techniques are all about combinatorial creativity (see Section 3.3), which is responsible for vast numbers of new ideas in all manner of fields. It is particularly useful if you want to bring in new voices from outside your team and take advantage of their differing views of the world. It also feels closest to most people's natural understanding of the creative process, so can be a good way to start brainstorming with a new or sceptical team.

Do this
Make a list of the people and organisations who've inspired you. Write down what you'd like to steal from them.

4.5 Break the rules

Identify as many rules as you can for the way your project should be done. Then break them one by one and see what you get. If you've been asked for radical new ideas, to think the unthinkable, this is the tool for you. If you need ideas that will surprise or stand out in a crowded market, these tools can deliver for you.

Rule-breaking tools take the things you've always done, all the things you think are essential, all the things everyone else is doing, and then work out the opposites.

See if any of these opposites inspire you to come up with new ideas for your project. You might feel uncomfortable using this tool at first, because it flies in the face of accepted wisdom. But give it a try: accepted wisdom was a new idea once.

Do this
Think of a brilliant idea that broke the rules. How did you feel when you first saw it?

Forced inspiration

4.6 Look harder inside the box

These tools start 'inside the box' and give you systematic ways to tinker with what you find there. These tools are inspired by the incremental nature of many new inventions and by the way we seem to find it easier to work backwards from form to function rather than the other way round.

You need to spend a good deal of your time working out exactly what you've got 'inside the box', so this is one approach which benefits from homework in advance.

These tools help you come up with lots of new shapes or forms for your project. You then work backwards to see what new functions these new forms could serve. This approach is less likely to throw up completely wacky ideas, so you may prefer to use it if you are working with a very senior (or not very playful) group.

> **Do this**
> How do you feel when asked to think 'outside the box'?

4.7 Brainwriting tools

With these tools you can generate hundreds of ideas in a short space of time. Yes, literally hundreds. You can use many of the other techniques working on your own, but brainwriting needs a group of people to build on each other's ideas.

Speed read

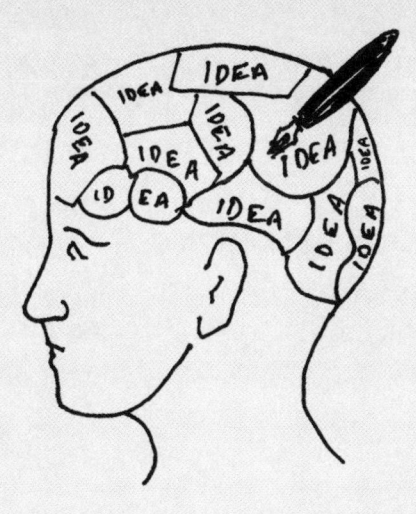

Each person starts with one or more simple ideas then swaps with others in the group, who build on their idea. Repeat the exercise three or four times and you rapidly build up several banks of ideas.

These techniques can stretch individuals in the team because they are inspired by ideas that have come from their colleagues. These tools usually require a period of silent working. This approach is particularly good for introverts and junior members of staff who might lack confidence to speak up in front of others.

Do this
Think about your last brainstorming session. Was it dominated by those who could speak loudest or with most confidence?

Tip
There are hundreds of excellent brainstorming techniques out there, freely available on different websites. I provide links to some of my favourites in my blog at www.newthinking.tools.

Remember: good techniques all demand time and space, provoke lateral and divergent thinking and are fun! You'll soon realise that generating lots of new ideas is the easy bit. Don't forget to leave enough time to discuss and converge on the strongest ideas.

BIG PICTURE
4. Forced inspiration

4.1 Brainstorm rules

Why

Search for 'brainstorm techniques' on the internet and you'll find dozens. Here's what the good ones have in common:

1. They all encourage divergent and lateral thinking.
2. They suspend normal judgement for a period.
3. Most of them feel playful.

Your search may also throw up some serious criticisms from people who think brainstorming is a waste of time. They're partly right: *badly run* brainstorms are an utter waste of everyone's time. So make sure you've got the right rules in place to run a good one.

Knowledge briefing

Ever since 'brainstorming' was invented in the 1940s, the practice has been criticised as unproductive compared to individuals working on their own (Kohn and Smith 2011). But while individuals may have ideas, it's groups or teams who put them into action. Well-managed brainstorms can build team cohesion and improve the flow of ideas. Team-working in scientific research has almost doubled in the past 50 years, and papers produced by teams tend to receive more citations than those produced by individuals (Wuchty *et al.* 2007).

How

1. Avoid the main pitfalls of bad brainstorms

This planning tool helps you prepare for your next brainstorm.

Weakness	Solution
Fixation: participants fix on weak ideas because they've been presented with flawed data or don't know enough about the subject.	Set 'homework' in advance so that everyone arrives at the session properly briefed with good data.
Free-riders: can sit back and let everyone else in a group do the work. People think there's nothing at stake and therefore don't take it seriously.	Break larger groups into subgroups of two to four people. It is much harder to free-ride in a smaller group. If people know they will have to share, test or pitch their ideas at the end of a session, they pay more attention.
Social matching: natural tendency for people to conform with peers and bosses.	Brainwriting techniques allow 'weaker' voices to be heard (Section 4.7). Devil's advocate techniques formalise dissent in a group (Section 6.3).
Safety first: people who think their ideas will be judged won't volunteer unusual or wild ideas.	Explicitly encourage wild ideas during the divergent or playful phase. Reassure more sceptical members of the group that wild ideas can be tamed in the convergent or serious phase.
Production blocking: hearing someone else's idea stops you realising your own.	Use silent techniques and small group discussions.
Cognitive overload: there's too much chatter for people to think clearly.	Build in plenty of breaks which allow people to 'incubate' their own ideas.

2. Set explicit rules for a good brainstorm

Send rules out in advance or read them out at the start of the session.

- *Have fun.* Laughter frees up the brain. Use a warm-up exercise to get the group laughing and moving around.
- *Go wild.* It's easier to find something useful in a wild idea than to inject life into a dull one. We'll look at how to tame wild ideas in Chapter 5.
- *Treat all ideas equally . . . at first.* If you respond positively to one idea, do the same for all. If you write down one idea, write them all down. Otherwise people will suspect you've got an agenda. Also, once ideas are written down it's easier to . . .
- *Build on other people's ideas.* Because two bad ideas can combine into a good one.
- *Take breaks.* Most people run out of steam after 20 or 30 minutes, or they get fixated on one idea. Take breaks and vary your techniques to keep everyone fresh.
- *Provide snacks.* Brain activity burns sugar!
- *Keep the door open.* People will keep having ideas after the brainstorm, so make sure they know how to pass them on to the right person.

Reflection

Think of the best brainstorm you've ever been in. What was the mood and feeling? What was the group dynamic? Did it generate new ideas? Now think of the worst. How was it different? What do you want to encourage and avoid in your session?

References

Kohn, N. and Smith, S.M. (2011) Collaborative fixation: Effects of others' ideas on brainstorming, *Applied Cognitive Psychology,* 25(3), 359–371.

Wuchty, S., Jones, B.F. and Uzzi, B. (2007) The increasing dominance of teams in the production of knowledge, *Science,* 316(5827): 1036–1039.

4.2 The lateral nudge and metaphor mash

Why

Metaphors surround us like the air we breathe. We use them constantly and to great effect. From early cave painting to modern road signs, from politics to psychotherapy, metaphors conjure up strong images in our minds.

If you can use image and metaphor to tap into our deep urge to find meaning, you are well on the way to generating unexpected new ideas.

Knowledge briefing

'The prime directive of the brain is to extract meaning' according to psychologist Peter Halligan, who has studied why people hold delusional beliefs. Our endless search for meaning can make us jump to the wrong conclusions but it can also help us jump to brilliant new ideas (New Scientist 2015). We are the only species that can live in a world of abstracts, vividly imagining past and future states or even things that can never exist. We build this world not out of words but out of *symbols and images*. This ability evolved in tandem with language (Deacon 1997).

Starting a creative process with images rather than words forces us to re-code the information we already have and 'map' it onto new symbols in our heads. Business adviser Kevin Duncan describes this as an 'analogy springboard' capable of launching us into endless sources of inspiration (Duncan 2014).

Big picture

How

1. The lateral nudge

- Group or solo exercise, 25 minutes. You'll need pens and paper, visual stimuli, for example, photocards available at www.newthinking.tools/downloads.

For this exercise:

- Set out the creative challenge.
- Split people into groups of two to four people and ask them to write down as many ideas as they can to address the challenge.
- After five minutes, stop them and hand out one photocard per person.
- Ask them to write down what that image could symbolise.
- Finally ask them to come up with one more idea each, inspired by their picture. Have an example ready: (this is a picture of a beach with storm clouds . . . could mean stormy times ahead . . . or summer holidays . . . or exploration . . . or silver linings . . . what storms could be ahead for your project?)

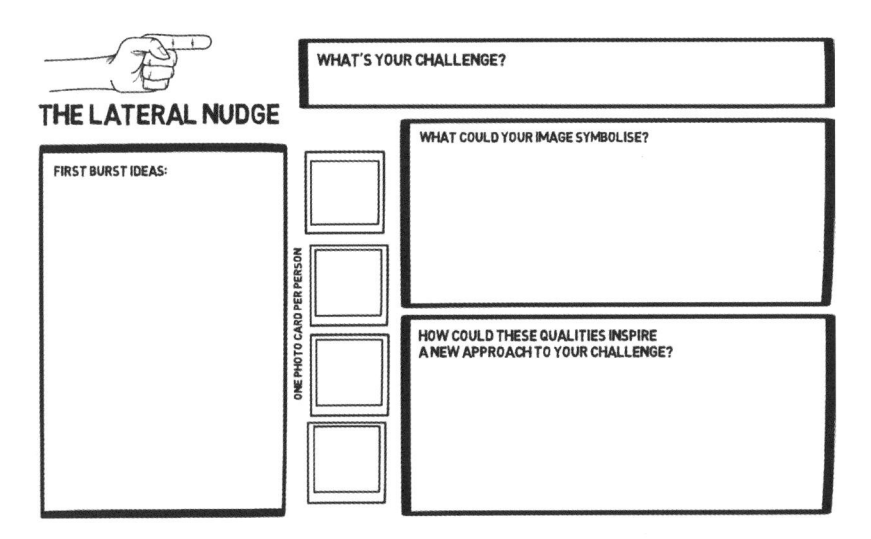

THE LATERAL NUDGE

FIRST BURST IDEAS:

WHAT'S YOUR CHALLENGE?

WHAT COULD YOUR IMAGE SYMBOLISE?

ONE PHOTO CARD PER PERSON

HOW COULD THESE QUALITIES INSPIRE A NEW APPROACH TO YOUR CHALLENGE?

Forced inspiration

With 10 minutes to go, ask the groups to choose their two favourite ideas and present them to the whole room. Use a convergent technique (Section 1.4) to pick the strongest idea.

Metaphor mash

- Group or solo exercise, 30–40 minutes. You'll need visual stimuli such as photocards or objects. Photocards available at www.newthinking.tools/downloads.

For this exercise:

- Give everyone a photo or object each.
- Ask everyone to work quietly on their own, writing down everything they can about their object: uses, shape, texture, what it reminds them of, could symbolise or stand for.
- Now ask them to turn to the person next to them and 'mash' their two images together to make a hybrid. Ask them what that hybrid could do, look like, symbolise etc. They should discuss this in pairs for a few minutes, and write down any new qualities that occur to them.
- Ask the pairs to choose their favourite qualities from any of the images they've looked at.
- Now do some lateral thinking: how could those qualities become the starting point or inspiration for their challenge?

With 10 minutes to go, ask the group to converge around the strongest ideas.

METAPHOR MASH

WHAT'S YOUR CHALLENGE?

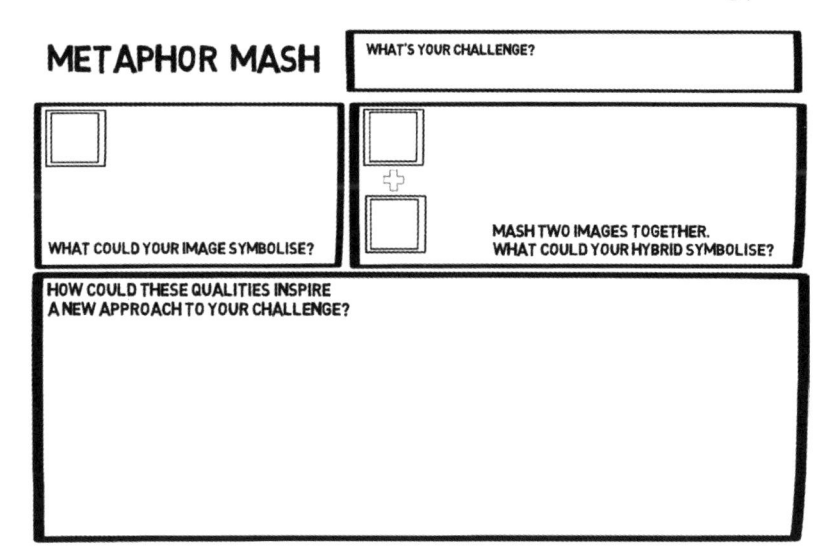

□	□
WHAT COULD YOUR IMAGE SYMBOLISE?	⊹ □ MASH TWO IMAGES TOGETHER. WHAT COULD YOUR HYBRID SYMBOLISE?

HOW COULD THESE QUALITIES INSPIRE A NEW APPROACH TO YOUR CHALLENGE?

Tip

It always helps to have a ready-made example in your back pocket to help people get the hang of what you're asking them to do.

- 'Here's a man walking his dog and a car crash. So the hybrid could be a disastrous dog walk . . . or guide dogs to keep us safe . . . or accident blind spots . . .'
- 'Let's take one of those: how could blind spots be an inspiration for our project?'
- 'What are our blind spots, what about our competitors, our customers?'

Reflection

Compare the ideas that came out in the first five minutes to the ones that came out after you introduced the lateral nudge. Which were the most original and surprising? How did the energy level in the room (the amount of chatter or laughter) change once you introduced the technique? How easy or difficult did people find it to move from metaphors to ideas?

References

Deacon, T. (1997) *The Symbolic Species: The Co-evolution of Language and the Human Brain.* Penguin.

Duncan, K. (2014) *The Ideas Book: 50 Ways to Generate Ideas More Effectively.* Lid Publishing.

New Scientist (2015) Are you deluded? The strange things we believe, *New Scientist,* 4 April.

4.3 Mapping your thoughts

Why

Ideas don't work in straight lines. They don't start at the beginning and end at the end. Different elements tumble over one another, collide, go sideways or backwards.

Mapping techniques accept that the creative process is nonlinear, especially at this stage, and they don't try to force ideas into straight lines or written documents before they're ready.

Knowledge briefing

The term 'mind mapping' was popularised by psychologist and author Tony Buzan in the 1970s, but the tradition of visually representing ideas as pictures, diagrams and webs goes through Walt Disney, Charles Darwin and Isaac Newton right back to 3rd-century philosophers.

Buzan argues that whatever our cultural background, our thinking combines imagination and multiple sensory associations. So we should use words, colours and pictures, with ideas radiating from a single central starting point in multiple branches (Buzan 2010).

As with other divergent thinking techniques (see Section 1.2), it's important to generate lots of branches on a map before trying to select the most useful. In this way, a mind map reflects the 'Darwinism of the synapses' which neuroscientists say accounts for our ability to learn and adapt our thinking (Simonton 1999).

Scientist Joseph D. Novak developed concept mapping as a tool for educators. Whereas a mind map radiates out from a central point, a concept map flows down a page from top to bottom, representing a hierarchy of connected ideas, where links show cause and effect. Novak also encouraged people to make cross-links between different domains (Novak 1998).

How

1. Mind map

- Group or solo exercise, 40–60 minutes.

For this exercise:

- Start with a single concept, question or statement in the centre of your paper. This allows ideas to expand in any direction.
- Draw branch lines radiating off representing each new related idea. You can make each branch a different colour. Use doodles as well as words to illustrate your branches.
- Be divergent: write down as many new branches as you can and keep going for at least two-thirds of your allotted time. Don't stop too soon and don't dwell for too long on any single branch.
- Once you have exhausted all your possible branches, take a step back and look at the overall picture. This will allow you to decide which are your top priorities and decide what to work on first.

Forced inspiration

- If you are working as a group, you can use a dot-vote system to pick out priorities or use the mind map to allocate tasks to the team.

This example looks at ideas around a workplace training programme

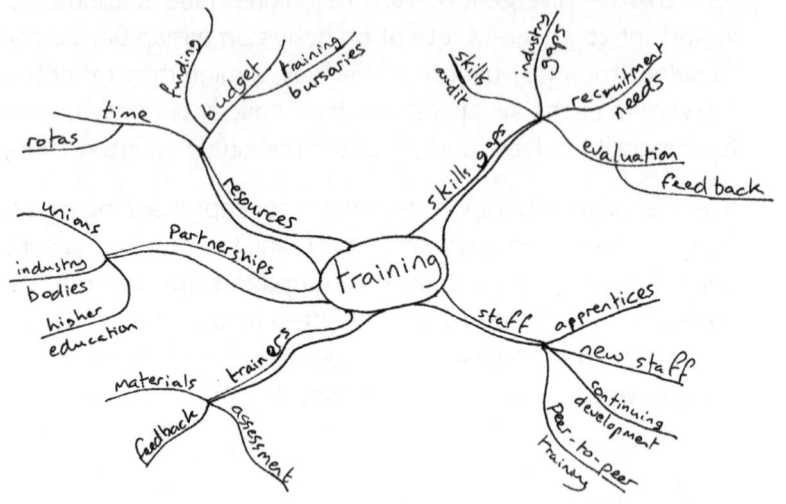

[Mind map centred on "training" with branches: funding, budget, training bursaries, time, rotas, resources, skills audit, skills gaps, industry gaps, recruitment needs, evaluation, feedback, unions, industry bodies, higher education, Partnerships, materials, trainers, feedback, assessment, staff, apprentices, new staff, continuing development, peer-to-peer training]

> **Tip**
> Although mind-mapping theory doesn't ask you to look for new connections between areas, you might find that obvious connections and themes emerge.

2. Concept map

- Group or solo exercise, 40–60 minutes. You'll need sticky notes.

For this exercise:

- Start by introducing the concept, statement or question about the project you're working on. Write this across the top of a large piece of paper or wall-space.
- Write down everything you can think of that relates to the domain or 'world' of your project or challenge. Write one item per sticky note.

Big picture

CONCEPT MAP

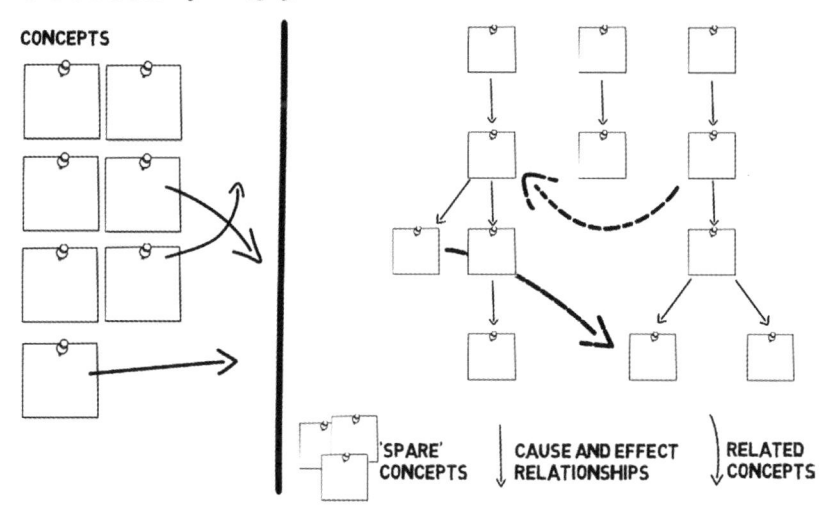

CONCEPTS

'SPARE' CONCEPTS | CAUSE AND EFFECT RELATIONSHIPS | RELATED CONCEPTS

- Now arrange the sticky notes underneath the main heading. Concept maps are hierarchical, so you should start with the most significant concepts and work downwards.
- Draw lines that explain the relationships between different concepts.
- Draw dotted lines for 'cross-links' that link one broad theme to another.
- If you can't fit some sticky notes into the map, keep them in view. They may show important gaps in your knowledge.
- Take a step back and decide which concepts and links are the most important. Assign tasks based on these priorities.

3. Multiple maps

- Solo and group exercise, at least four hours. You'll need a large room.

This technique, designed by US consultant Carl Selfe, builds individual maps into a group map. At each stage there is debate on what should be prioritised and left out.

Forced inspiration

- Solo ideas: each individual creates their own map.
- Small groups (two to four people): create a new map incorporating all the branches of the individual maps without deciding priorities.
- Take a break. Encourage people to wander round with their tea/coffee looking at the maps.
- Small group debate: decide on priorities. Redraw map using only these priorities, prune back the rest.
- Large group: incorporate all the branches of the small group maps into a new map, without discussing priorities.
- Take a break. Wander the room looking at the maps.
- Large group debate: work out which elements are most important and create a final map combining only the top priorities which have emerged.

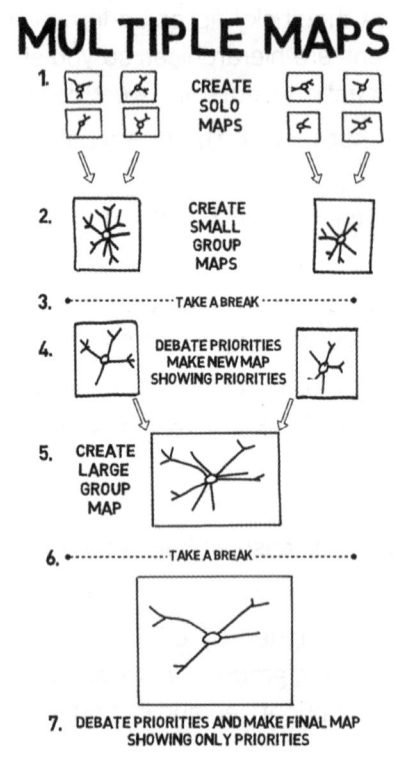

MULTIPLE MAPS

1. CREATE SOLO MAPS
2. CREATE SMALL GROUP MAPS
3. TAKE A BREAK
4. DEBATE PRIORITIES MAKE NEW MAP SHOWING PRIORITIES
5. CREATE LARGE GROUP MAP
6. TAKE A BREAK
7. DEBATE PRIORITIES AND MAKE FINAL MAP SHOWING ONLY PRIORITIES

Source: Based on a technique designed by Carle Selfe.

Reflection

Whatever kind of map you're using, put it up on display in your working area. You will be amazed how many times you come back to it as a source of inspiration.

References

Buzan, T. (2010) *The Mind Map Book: Unlock Your Creativity, Boost Your Memory, Change Your Life.* Pearson.

Novak, J.D. (1998) *Learning, Creating and Using Knowledge: Concept Maps as Facilitative Tools for Schools and Corporations.* Routledge.

Selfe, C.K. (n.d.) *Brainstorming Research Elements as a Team by Mind Mapping.* The Proposal Centres. See http://tinyurl.com/CarlSelfMaps for details.

Simonton, K. (1999) *Origins of Genius: Darwinian Perspectives on Creativity.* Oxford University Press.

4.4 Steal from the heart

Why

To copy, to plagiarise, to be inspired by – what's the difference? Well, the first is slavish and the second is sneaky; only the third is truly creative.

We all learn our craft from the example of others, whether this is picking out chords from favourite songs as we learn the guitar or following best practice as we join a profession. Inevitably we want to be inspired by the best we see around us.

What sets these techniques apart from simple copying – or sneaky plagiarism – is the desire to steal the essence of what's inspired us, not just the outward form. As artist and writer Austin Kleon says: 'Don't just steal the style, steal the thinking behind the style. You don't want to look like your heroes, you want to see like them.'

Knowledge briefing

The history of invention is awash with examples of creative stealing, also described as 'combinatorial creativity' (Csikszentmihalyi 1996; Klein 2014; Johnson 2010).

Most of us seem to find it much easier to work backwards from form to function and not the other way round. It's easier to see something brilliant and imagine adapting it to a new function than it is to start with a problem and try to imagine a new solution (Boyd and Goldenberg 2013).

Scientist Anthony McCaffrey realised that most successful inventors do two things. They notice a commonly overlooked part of a problem, then design a solution for it. Often they find solutions ready-made in different fields from their own. McCaffrey's Automated Innovation software breaks problems down into component parts, then searches patent records for anyone who has found solutions to related problems (McCaffrey 2013). You can steal creatively by using words that belong to something else. Describing a problem in new terms can prompt our brains to find new solutions (Allan *et al.* 2002).

How

1. Steal from the heart

- Group or solo exercise, 40 minutes.

For this exercise:

- Start by deciding what is at the heart of your creative challenge or project.

Big picture

- Now ask yourself who is brilliant at doing those things that are at the heart of your project. The first suggestions will always be the obvious ones, so keep going and make a long list of 'who is brilliant?'
- Next, take one of these examples of brilliance and ask what qualities make them brilliant. Make a long list of all the qualities you can think of. Repeat this process with more cases of 'who is brilliant?' until you have a long list of qualities.
- Now ask how you could apply the qualities in this list to the challenge you are working on.

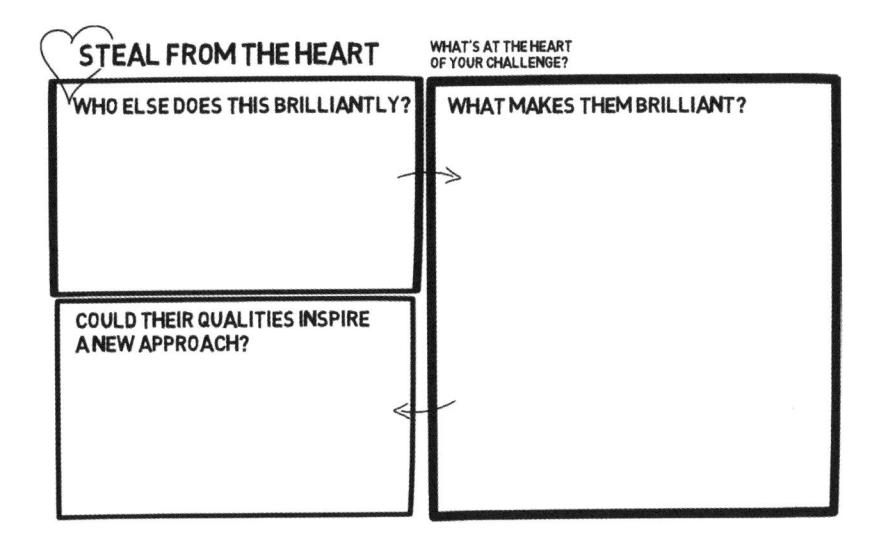

STEAL FROM THE HEART — WHAT'S AT THE HEART OF YOUR CHALLENGE?

WHO ELSE DOES THIS BRILLIANTLY?	WHAT MAKES THEM BRILLIANT?
COULD THEIR QUALITIES INSPIRE A NEW APPROACH?	

Keep going until you have only 10 minutes left in your session. Finally, ask people to use a convergent technique to choose the ideas you want to take forward (see Section 1.4).

> **Tip**
> This technique won't work unless you get really diverse examples of brilliance. If you just list the brilliant people doing the same work as your project, then your second list – qualities that make them brilliant – will be pretty obvious.

Forced inspiration

2. Steal from a thesaurus

- Group or solo exercise, 50 minutes. You'll need a thesaurus (print or online version).

This tool blends Anthony McCaffrey's (2013) computer search with Allan et al.'s (2002) re-expression technique.

- Start by writing out a list of the key components of your project or the creative challenge you are trying to solve, using one sticky note per word. Keep going until you have described every aspect of the problem.
- Pick one sticky note, put it onto the top of a separate piece of paper. Now grab your thesaurus and write as many different synonyms (words that have the same, or close to the same, meaning) as the word on the sticky note.
- Pick out one synonym. Ask yourself who has solved a problem related to it. Repeat this process with other words from your list of components, making a new list of synonyms and searching for related solutions.
- Think of how you could relate those solutions to your problem, writing down a list of new ideas. With 10 minutes left, ask the group to pick out the most promising ideas and decide priorities (convergent thinking – see Section 1.4).

An example of the 'steal from a thesaurus' technique applied to the challenge of setting up a new workplace training programme

STEAL FROM THE THESAURUS

1. YOUR CHALLENGE	2. SYNONYMS	3. RELATED SOLUTIONS	4. NEW IDEAS
courses	training	drill	how can we have 'live fire' exercises?
training	coaching	firing range	
	discipline	army recruits	which skills should be automatic?
trainers	drill	parade drill	
staff	education	basic training	how do teams hand over knowledge to each other?
tests	exercise	debriefing	
	tuition	officer training	

Reflection

How many new ideas have you worked on already that were, in fact, adapted from previous examples of brilliance? Consider how you feel when you see another person or organisation come up with a brilliant idea. Which of their qualities do you wish you had?

References

Allan, D., Kingdon, M., Murrin, K. and Rudkin, D. (2002) *Sticky Wisdom: How to Start a Creative Revolution at Work.* ?WhatIf! Publications.
Boyd, D. and Goldenberg, J. (2013) *Inside the Box: Why the Best Business Innovations Are Right in Front of You.* Profile Books.
Csikszentmihalyi, M. (1996) *Creativity: The Psychology of Discovery and Invention.* HarperCollins.
Johnson, S. (2010) *Where Good Ideas Come From: The Natural History of Innovation.* Penguin Books.
Klein, G. (2014) *Seeing What Others Don't: The Remarkable Ways We Gain Insights.* Nicholas Brealey Publishing.
McCaffrey, A. (2013) www.innovationaccelerator.com

4.5 Break the rules

Why

Rule breakers, rebels and mavericks: they can be the poster boys and girls of the innovative business world. They can also be uncomfortable to work with, disruptive and a cause of conflict.

Rules exist for a reason: to get predictable results, safely delivered on time. We'd think twice before choosing to fly with a maverick airline pilot or go under the knife of a rebel brain surgeon. But whatever business we're in, it's good to challenge the way we operate. Rule-breaking techniques turn the world upside down – in the safety of a brainstorm.

Knowledge briefing

Our brains love to impose order on chaos, so we constantly create rules to explain what is happening around us. If those rules appear to make sense, we stick to them (De Bono 1970). We are also used to arranging ideas into categories, each with its own set of rules. Unless we deliberately challenge this process, we tend to see emerging ideas in old terms (Allan *et al.* 2002).

Rule-breaking immediately gains attention. We are hardwired to notice anomalies and contradictions (Kahneman 2011). So in a busy world, a rule-breaking message, product or service can cut through the clutter.

'Doing the opposite is an exercise worth trying,' says copywriter Pete Barry. 'At worst you'll produce something different and unexpected but useless. At best, it can be brilliant, inspiring and even revolutionary' (Barry 2008).

How

1. Break every rule

- Group or solo exercise, 40–50 minutes. Worksheets optional.

For this exercise:

- Remind everyone of your creative challenge. Write down a list of all the rules that normally apply. Ask: 'What do we always do? What do we always have?'
- Start at the top of the list and ask: 'What are the opposites to this rule?' Note that I said 'opposites' plural. With the example of a workplace training scheme: we always have expert trainers. So

Big picture

BREAK THE RULES | WHAT'S YOUR CHALLENGE?

1. HOW DO WE ALWAYS DO THIS?

2. WHAT ARE THE OPPOSITES?

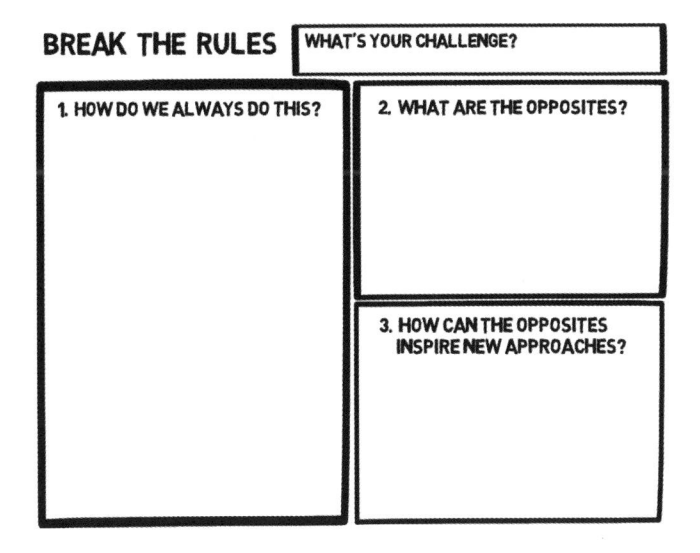

3. HOW CAN THE OPPOSITES INSPIRE NEW APPROACHES?

what are the opposites of expert trainers? No trainers. Yes, what else? Amateur trainers ... practitioners ... apprentices ... members of the public ... idiots ...

- Look at your list of opposites – which can inspire new ideas? Some are just plain bad. You're not going to employ idiots to run training sessions (but you might want to make them foolproof). Amateur trainers? Well, that could mean peer-to-peer training. Apprentices ... could they teach their social media skills to older staff? And so on. Choose the strongest ideas to take forward.

Tip
Breaking the most obvious rule, the one thing that everyone thinks is indispensable, can produce the most creative ideas. Don't let anything be off limits.

2. Mission impossible[6]
- Group or solo exercise, 30–40 minutes. Worksheet optional.

---
[6] This technique is from Gray *et al.* (2010).

Forced inspiration

For this exercise:

- Remind everyone of your challenge. Write a list of the constraints you would normally expect to operate within (e.g. budget, staffing, resources, timing).
- Take one of those constraints and tighten it up until it becomes Mission Impossible:
  - How could we deliver this in one day?
  - How could we do this for zero cost?
  - How could we do this with no additional staff?
- If you get an immediate 'That's impossible!' response, ask people to think who or what they'd have to call on to achieve the mission despite the extreme constraints.
- When you've exhausted your first set of options, take another constraint and tighten that instead. Repeat the process.
- With 10 minutes to go, ask people to review the options that have emerged. Are any of them viable or worth investigating? Have you tapped into hidden resources?
- Choose the strongest ideas you want to take forward.

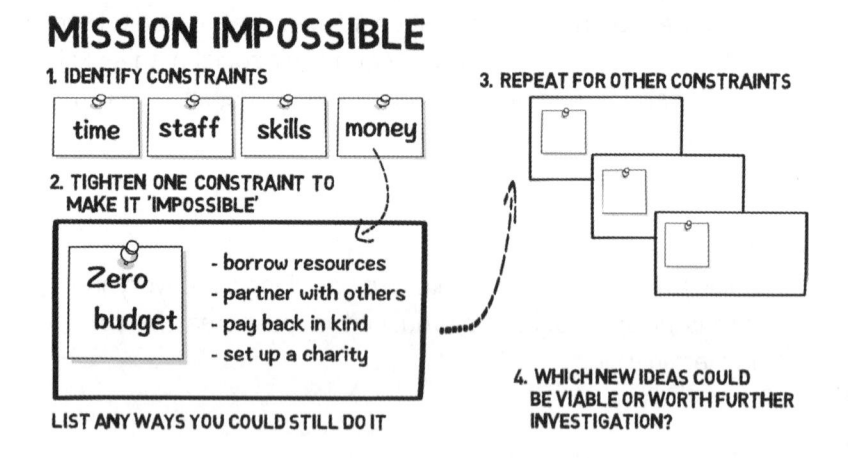

MISSION IMPOSSIBLE

1. IDENTIFY CONSTRAINTS

| time | staff | skills | money |

2. TIGHTEN ONE CONSTRAINT TO MAKE IT 'IMPOSSIBLE'

Zero budget
- borrow resources
- partner with others
- pay back in kind
- set up a charity

LIST ANY WAYS YOU COULD STILL DO IT

3. REPEAT FOR OTHER CONSTRAINTS

4. WHICH NEW IDEAS COULD BE VIABLE OR WORTH FURTHER INVESTIGATION?

Reflection

Breaking the rules is hard for some people, especially if they've written those rules. So remind everyone that this is a playful, experimental phase in the creative process. You may need to agree some rules on confidentiality if you're about to break into taboo areas.

References

Allan, D., Kingdon, M., Murrin, K. and Rudkin, D. (2002) *Sticky Wisdom: How to Start a Creative Revolution at Work.* ?WhatIf! Publications.
Barry, P. (2008) *The Advertising Concept Book: A Complete Guide to Creative Ideas, Strategies and Campaigns.* Thames & Hudson.
De Bono, E. (1970) *Lateral Thinking.* Penguin Books.
Gray, D., Brown S. and Macanufo, J. (2010) *Gamestorming. A Playbook for Innovators, Rulebreakers and Changemakers.* O'Reilly.
Kahneman, D. (2011) *Thinking, Fast and Slow.* Penguin Books.

4.6 Look harder inside the box

Why

The phrase 'thinking outside the box' comes from a nine-dot puzzle that can only be solved by ignoring the obvious box-like shape created by the dots. The term has become a business cliche, especially for anyone talking about the creative process. Whatever force it once had is weakened by repetition. Personally, I cringe every time I hear it.

'Outside the box' for some people means wild, crazy and unworkable ideas. If you take the phrase literally, you can see why.

If everything you know about a problem is inside the box, along with all your experience, expertise and understanding, how can you possibly think outside it? Why would you want to?

The tools in this section are about staying *inside the box*. They encourage you to look with fresh eyes at what's there and see what happens if you rearrange things. They push you right up to the edge of the possible – right to the edge of the box.

Knowledge briefing

Several systems of innovation focus on what's 'inside the box' for a particular project or industry. Back in the 1970s, Edward M. Tauber designed a heuristic ideation technique for the food industry, based on the heuristic (or rule of thumb) that many innovations came from novel combinations of two unrelated factors inside the same industry (Tauber 1972).

Drew Boyd and Jacob Goldenberg argue that simple templates for exploring and reconfiguring what's inside the box can generate lots of new forms. We can then work out if those new forms have any useful functions. Often solutions lie very close to hand, in the 'closed world' surrounding the problem we're struggling with (Boyd and Goldenberg 2013).

Educator Bob Eberle took several questions commonly used in brainstorming and organised them into SCAMPER as a way of shaking up the contents of your box. This mnemonic asks you to Substitute, Combine, Adapt, Modify, Put to another use, Eliminate or Rearrange elements of a product or service (Eberle 2008).

How

1. Subtraction

- Group or solo exercise, 50 minutes. You'll need sticky notes; worksheet optional.

Based on *Inside the Box* by Drew Boyd and Jacob Goldenberg (2013).

Big picture

- List all the elements of your project (people, resources etc.) writing each one on a separate sticky note. Stick them on a piece of paper and draw a box around them.
- Now write around the box all the factors (people and resources) that are not part of your project but are close to hand. These form the 'closed world' immediately around your project.
- Try a *simple subtraction*: take away one sticky note at a time, removing a factor you previously thought was essential to your project. Ask yourself what benefits the slimmed-down version could bring. Who might want it and why? Is it viable?
- Now *subtract* and *substitute*: take away one factor from inside the box. What are the benefits of the slimmed-down version? Look at the closed world immediately surrounding the box. Is there anything here that would fill the gap left by the feature you've removed?
- Are any of the new ideas viable? Repeat the task, using a different piece from the box.

INSIDE THE BOX - SUBTRACTION

1. INSIDE THE BOX	2. THE 'CLOSED WORLD' IMMEDIATELY AROUND THE BOX
3. SIMPLE SUBTRACTION TAKE ONE FEATURE AWAY WHAT ARE THE BENEFITS?	4. SUBTRACT AND SUBSTITUTE REPLACE MISSING FEATURE FROM 'CLOSED WORLD' WHAT ARE THE BENEFITS?

Here's an example of simple subtraction. In order to make a cheaper phone, Motorola removed the transmitter from one model. The Mango could receive but not make calls. Who would want a cheap phone that couldn't make calls? Well, it turned out parents of pre-teen children did, so too did managers of out-of-office sales teams. Mango went on to take 5 per cent of the market in Israel where it launched.[7]

Let's take the example of a workplace training challenge. Let's subtract something at the heart of the project: the trainees themselves. It would certainly be less disruptive if you weren't dragging staff away to training schemes. What could replace trainees from the closed world around you? How about customers? What would it mean if you trained key customers, made them more aware of your products? How could you benefit? What could you learn from them?

2. Scamper[8]

- Group or solo exercise, 90 minutes. You'll need sticky notes; worksheet optional.

For this exercise:

- Start by listing all the elements of your project or creative challenge, writing each one on a separate sticky note.
- Take sticky notes one at a time or in batches and put them through the SCAMPER list. If you are working in a large group, split people up and let each subgroup use SCAMPER in different ways.
- With 10 minutes to go, ask people to choose the options that they think are most viable and converge around the ideas you want to take forward.

Here's an example – putting ideas for workplace training schemes through SCAMPER.

---

[7] From Boyd and Goldenberg (2013).
[8] Adapted from Eberle (2008).

INSIDE THE BOX - SCAMPER

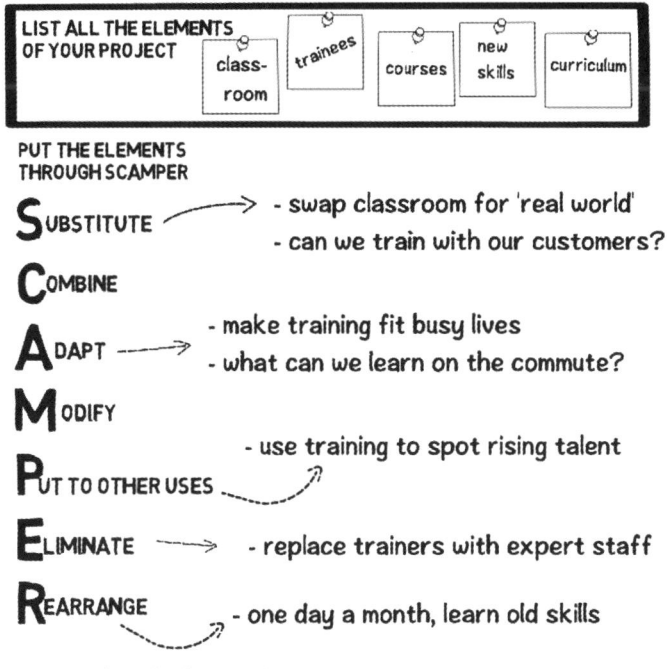

LIST ALL THE ELEMENTS OF YOUR PROJECT: classroom, trainees, courses, new skills, curriculum

PUT THE ELEMENTS THROUGH SCAMPER

SUBSTITUTE
- swap classroom for 'real world'
- can we train with our customers?

COMBINE

ADAPT
- make training fit busy lives
- what can we learn on the commute?

MODIFY

PUT TO OTHER USES
- use training to spot rising talent

ELIMINATE → - replace trainers with expert staff

REARRANGE - one day a month, learn old skills

Source: Based on Eberle (2008).

Reflection

How do these techniques compare to the more freewheeling approach of lateral nudge and metaphor mash (Section 4.2)? Did people resist the idea of throwing away something you all thought was essential to the project?

References

Boyd, D. and Goldenberg, J. (2013) *Inside the Box: Why the Best Business Innovations Are Right in Front of You.* Profile Books.

Eberle, B. (2008) *SCAMPER: Creative Games and Activities for Imagination Development.* Prufrock Press.

Tauber, E.M. (1972) Heuristic ideation technique: A systematic procedure for new product search, *Journal of Marketing*, 36(1), 58–61.

4.7 Brainwriting tools

Why

If your experience of brainstorming has been a freewheeling session, where people shout ideas, then brainwriting tools will push you in a different direction. They give people a chance to think silently, to reflect on their own thoughts, without being swayed by the loudest voice in the room. These techniques are perfect for groups which tend to dominated by the same old voices, where you need to level the playing field between junior and senior members, or bring in diverse new voices.

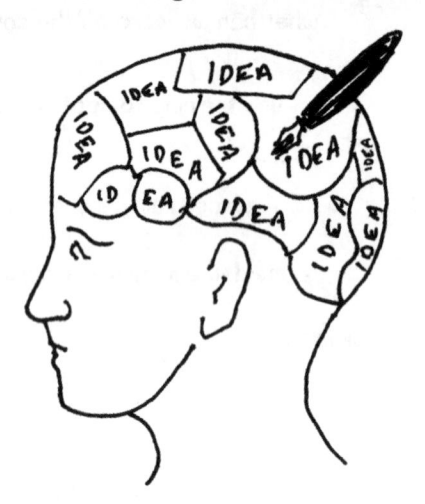

Brainwriting tools help with lateral thinking, as your ideas are shaped by what's inside someone else's head. These tools can produce hundreds of ideas. This means you must leave enough time to converge effectively on the best ideas.

Knowledge briefing

In a free-flowing group discussion, people can bounce ideas off each other in new and exciting ways. However, our brains struggle to listen to what others are saying *while simultaneously* hatching our own ideas. So we either stop listening and jump in with our own ideas, or let the strongest voice in the room sway our thoughts (Diehl and Stroebe, 1991).

Brainwriting tools combine silent working – so individuals can think straight – with regular exchange of ideas within a group. There is evidence that this method results in greater productivity compared to individuals working on their own or in an unstructured group discussion (Paulus and Yang 2000). Silent techniques also encourage contributions from more introverted members of a group who may lack the confidence to voice the germ of a new idea in front of their peers (Cain 2013).

How

1. Brainwriting sheets

- Group exercise, 30–40 minutes. You'll need sheets of A4 paper with nine-box grids drawn on.

This technique was designed by Horst Geschka in 1979.

- Start with several blank sheets of A4 paper. Always have one more sheet than the number of people in your group. Remind people of your creative challenge. Then ask them to write their first three ideas in the top row, one idea per box. This is a silent technique, so no discussion is allowed.
- The first individual to finish a line of three boxes puts their page into the middle of the table and picks up the remaining blank sheet and starts again with three more ideas. Everyone else swaps sheets when they finish, picking up a free sheet from the centre. All of these sheets now have other people's ideas written on them. Ask them to *build on the ideas* they pick up, writing new ideas in the second row of boxes.
- As people finish their second line, they swap again. This time they are building on any of the six boxes of ideas on the sheet they pick up.
- When all the boxes are filled in, the exercise ends. Everyone swaps sheets one last time. Give people at least five minutes to read *all* the ideas on their page.
- Converge by asking them to nominate their favourite ideas from their page. If you need to keep novelty alive, ask them

Forced inspiration

BRAINWRITING

1. FILL IN TOP THREE BOXES

2. READ FIRST THREE IDEAS AND BUILD THREE NEW IDEAS

SWAP YOUR PAPER WITH SOMEONE ELSE

4. SWAP AGAIN. READ ALL NINE IDEAS. DISCUSS WHICH IDEAS ARE STRONGEST

3. SWAP AGAIN. READ FIRST SIX IDEAS AND BUILD THREE NEW IDEAS

for one practical idea and one wild idea they really like. Write these up on a flip chart and decide which ideas to take forward.

2. Floor-walking

- Group exercise, 40–50 minutes. You'll need large sheets of paper/flip charts, sticky notes and a room with plenty of space to move around.

Big picture

This is a variation on classic brainwriting which moves *people* rather than paper. This gets everyone up on their feet, which gets blood flowing to their brains.

- Arrange large sheets of paper – one per person if possible – around the table or on walls around the room. Explain your creative challenge and ask people to write their first idea at the top of the paper. This is a silent exercise, so no discussion.
- When they've finished, they move on to another paper, read the idea written on it and build on it, writing a new idea underneath.

- Faster writers use sticky notes to avoid a log-jam behind slower writers.
- Keep people moving until all the pages are filled, or until you only have 15 minutes left in your session.
- Use a convergent technique such as dot-voting (see Section 1.4) to choose the strongest ideas to take forward.

Reflection

Did you notice how quiet it goes during the brainwriting session? This is because people are thinking hard. Interrupt this silence as little as possible.

Brainwriting techniques really get moving once you start *building on other people's ideas*. So encourage people not to put too much time or detail into their first ideas.

References

Cain, S. (2013) *Quiet: The Power of Introverts in a World that Can't Stop Talking.* Penguin Books.

Diehl, M. and Stroebe, W. (1991) Productivity loss in idea-generating groups: Tracking down the blocking effect, *Journal of Personality and Social Psychology,* 61(3): 392–403.

Geschka, H. (1979) Methods and organisations of idea generation. Creativity Week Two. *1979 Proceedings.* Centre for Creative Leadership.

Paulus, P.B. and Yang, H-C. (2000) Idea generation in groups: A basis for creativity in organisations, *Organisational Behaviour and Human Decision Processes,* 82(1), 76–87.

Chapter 5

Nurture good ideas

5.1 The developer's dilemma

5.2 Supportive teams

5.3 Widen your pool of talent

5.4 Design thinking

5.5 Keep the novelty alive

5.6 Working with wild ideas

5.7 Moving out of the greenhouse

SPEED READ
5. Nurture good ideas

5.1 The developer's dilemma

How new can your new ideas really be? If they're too revolutionary, they'll be seen as a long shot and you may struggle to find backers. If they're too safe, you've got a better chance of success but you'll fail to excite. This is the developer's dilemma.

New ideas need nurturing or else they die young. At the inspiration stage all you've got is the seed of an idea. Scatter those on the ground and you'll be lucky if a handful make it to full grown plants. The development stage is like the greenhouse, where you give the seeds a chance to grow, safe from frost and away from choking weeds.

So whether you are trying for incremental change or radical overhaul, you have to nurture and support new ideas before selecting the best. If an idea doesn't work, despite the best efforts of the developers, then chuck it out of the greenhouse. But make sure to learn the lessons from what went wrong.

Finally, we mustn't leave ideas in development for too long, or the greenhouse becomes totally overgrown. Every idea, like every plant, must eventually withstand harsh reality.

Nurture good ideas

Do this
Think how you react when someone suggests a new idea. Do you nurture it or want to see if it'll thrive straight away?

5.2 Supportive teams

Ideas occur in an individual's mind, but it's teams who usually deliver them. Nobody's idea is perfect at first, and it can be embarrassing to share incomplete work in front of others. You need to find a way to take the emotional sting out of the development stage if you're going to get a team to support each other.

Testing an idea in the development stage may throw up concerns about your entire project. This can cause problems; however, you can use these insights to make your overall project stronger.

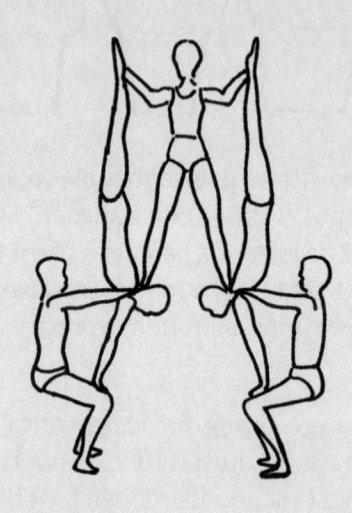

Do this
Think about how you feel if you have to share incomplete work with others. How do you react when someone shares half-formed ideas with you?

Speed read

5.3 Widen your pool of talent

Some of the biggest names in the corporate world open up their creative processes beyond a small development team. If you can find the right collaborators and manage the process well, you can multiply your collective brain power massively. Open innovation flourishes on the web, channelling expertise from all over the world to the right creative challenges.

You might be able to fish from a wider pool of development talent and find outsiders who know your project almost as well as you do. Amateurs and consumers can be a valuable resource.

Do this
Think of the online communities who discuss your kind of work. Do they contain a different kind of expertise that you could use?

5.4 Design thinking

Good design doesn't just mean letting some 'creatives' polish up a product once the engineers have finished building it. Design thinking, with its love of prototyping and its tolerance of failures, can make the idea better in the first place.

The mass production age meant expensive factory lines, which in turn meant new products had to be as close to perfect as possible before production started. Failure meant product recall.

Nurture good ideas

The flexible nature of modern production and delivery allows producers to experiment with beta versions, carry out live testing and adopt a 'fail fast' philosophy. Even if you don't work in digital industries, you can still use design thinking to strengthen the way you develop ideas.

> **Do this**
> Think back to a project that failed when you tested it. What was your attitude to failure? What about others in your workplace? What did you learn?

5.5 Keep the novelty alive

How many times have you worked for people who say they want risky, radical ideas, but play it safe when you come up with one? When the stakes are high, we are loss averse and have a natural tendency to take the safe option.

Often we say this is gut instinct or on-the-job experience coming into play. We tell ourselves we can 'just see' which ideas are going to work. This may be true, or it may be a little voice from inside your comfort zone, trying to steer you towards the less risky option.

Speed read

You can keep the novelty alive in a new idea by praising its good points and potential first, before looking constructively at its weaknesses.

> **Do this**
> Have you ever played it safe, only to wish later you'd taken a risk on a new idea? Have you seen this happen to your ideas? What were the arguments against taking the risk?

5.6 Working with wild ideas

A common criticism of badly run brainstorms is that they only produce unworkable ideas. If your creative process only delivers a bunch of wild ideas, you are wasting everyone's time. You're also making it less likely that people will take you seriously next time. But you don't want to go to the other extreme and crush an idea which has got everyone excited, just because you can't see a practical way forward.

Nurture good ideas

You can work with a wild idea by exploring what you can do with it, rather than how much you can't. You can focus on the novelty that might excite your customers or audience, rather than the difficulties your production team might see.

The wild idea might not turn out to be so impractical after all. Or it might be a stepping stone that connects you to a new but more workable alternative.

> **Do this**
> Think of a brainstorm where a wild idea came out. What happened to the idea?

5.7 Moving out of the greenhouse

You've brainstormed your new ideas, you've tested and nurtured them in the greenhouse. Now it's time to move the best of them out into the big, wide world.

The early stages of the creative process have been about divergent thinking: multiplying your options. Now it's time to close options down and choose the one you're going to put your time, effort and reputation behind. You're at the ultimate convergent thinking stage. It's time to move out of the greenhouse.

Speed read

You can rely on gut instinct at this stage: ask yourself what 'just feels' like the best option. Or you can apply creative techniques and make your decision transparent to those around you.

Finally, no matter how nurturing you want to be, there'll be times when you need to kill a new idea that isn't working. The trick is to do this without crushing the creative spark that will ignite the next new idea.

Do this
Think about how ideas get final approval where you work. Does it appear to be on gut instinct or are the reasons behind the decisions clear?

BIG PICTURE
5. Nurture good ideas

5.1 The developer's dilemma

Why

When you're in the early stages of brainstorming, excited about your new ideas, it's worth reminding yourself, as Robert Poynton puts it:

> 'There's no such thing as a good idea . . . yet.'

'Early on, *all* of our movies suck,' according to Ed Catmull, the man who founded Pixar. Our job as developers, he says, is to make them go 'from suck to non-suck'."

This takes us to the heart of the developer's dilemma: how long do you work on an idea before deciding if it's the right one? The more radical your idea, the more odd and unworkable it will seem at first. But if an idea looks workable straight away, it probably isn't very original.

All new ideas need a period of nurturing in a supportive environment. You need to treat them like seedlings and put them in a greenhouse, rather than just scatter them on the ground and hope for the best.

Knowledge briefing

The consultants at ?WhatIf! creative agency contrast the development phase with the urgent demands of business as usual. They say one looks like a greenhouse while the other resembles the emergency room in a busy hospital.

Nurture good ideas

Working in a greenhouse needs a different mindset from the emergency room. This should be signalled clearly, otherwise seedling ideas will wither before they've had a chance to show their potential (Allan *et al.* 2002).

Pixar established a Brains Trust, a place where senior directors and writers give truly candid feedback on each other's work as a movie takes shape. Crucially, no-one in the Brains Trust has the authority to make their views stick. They speak frankly, ask questions and make suggestions to the director in charge (Catmull and Wallace 2014).

The BBC recently opened up some of its traditionally secretive development processes, setting up its own online greenhouse space called Taster. Anyone in the UK can test, rate and comment on the work in progress. 'Not everything will work, some things might break. This is potentially hard for an organisation that prides itself on always being highest quality,' says the head of the BBC's R&D lab at MediaCityUK, Adrian Woolard. 'But we learn quicker about what won't work, saving money and improving the final proposition.' After three months, pilots are taken out of Taster and rigorously evaluated (Woolard 2015).

Deadlines are vital. Nobody wants their ideas to be stuck in what Hollywood writers call 'development hell', limping along, damned by faint interest. The UK government set up its Behavioural Insights Team (aka the 'Nudge Unit') complete with a sunset clause: if the team hadn't proved its worth after two years, it would be scrapped (Halpern 2015).

Big picture

How

1. Greenhouse behaviour[9]

- Group or solo exercise, 30–40 minutes. Worksheet optional.

Take your new idea and put it through ?WhatIf!'s greenhouse behaviour guide for SUN and RAIN thinking. I've used the example of a project to create video tutorials for your workplace training programme.

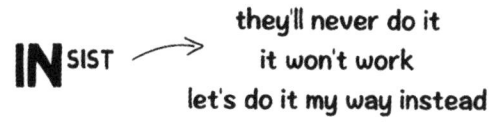

RAIN AND SUN

REACT — sounds expensive
that's going to be tricky

ASSUME — video tutorials don't work
we've tried this before

INSIST — they'll never do it
it won't work
let's do it my way instead

Source: Based on Allan *et al.* (2002).

Now put your project idea through the RAIN
React
Assume
INsist

---

[9] This technique is from Allan *et al.* (2002).

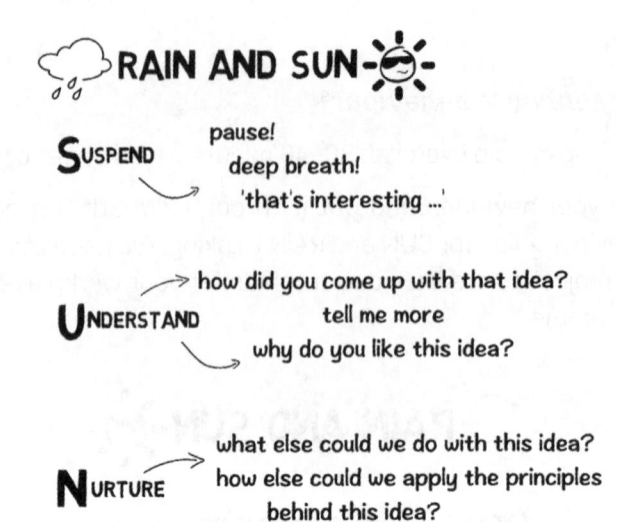

Nurture good ideas

☁ RAIN AND SUN ☀

SUSPEND → pause!
deep breath!
'that's interesting ...'

UNDERSTAND → how did you come up with that idea?
tell me more
why do you like this idea?

NURTURE → what else could we do with this idea?
how else could we apply the principles behind this idea?

Source: Based on Allan *et al.* (2002).

Now see what happens when you put your project idea into the SUN
Suspend your judgement
Understand
Nurture

2. Brains Trust behaviour

How can you set up a forum for candid criticism like Pixar's Brains Trust? This is what Pixar boss Ed Catmull would say about making it work:

- Recruit people who understand and care about your project.
- Ask them to critique the idea, not the person.
- Look for 'frank talk, spirited debate, laughter and love'.
- Don't give them any official authority.

3. Timing

Set a deadline or a sunset clause, so that your idea doesn't limp on forever in development. Evaluate what you've achieved, celebrate the successes and share lessons from the failures.

Reflection

What kind of pressure are you under to deliver fully fledged ideas at the start of your creative process? Is that coming from you or others?

References

Allan, D., Kingdon, M., Murrin, K. and Rudkin, D. (2002) *Sticky Wisdom: How to Start a Creative Revolution at Work.* ?WhatIf! Publications.

Catmull, E. and Wallace, A. (2014) *Creativity, Inc. Overcoming the Unseen Forces that Stand in the Way of True Inspiration.* Bantam Press.

Halpern, D. (2015) *Inside the Nudge Unit: How Small Changes Can Make a Big Difference.* W.H. Allen.

Woolard, A. (2015) BBC Taster: first week: http://tinyurl.com/bbctaster

5.2 Supportive teams

Why

The culture of your workplace shapes how creative you can be there. This applies from the way you are led to how your team works together. Leaders of successful creative workplaces put a great deal of time into getting the culture right.

Often, cultural norms are not written down anywhere. It's commonly accepted by people who've been around a while that this is how things are done – or not done – around here. This is inevitable in a busy working environment. But it doesn't stop you creating new rules based on what innovative teams do elsewhere.

Knowledge briefing

Good development teams foster trust between colleagues, based on the knowledge that no idea is perfect at first. Teams have to learn to avoid quick judgements or rushing to action during the development stage. It's better to respond with questions instead, as this helps the new idea grow stronger (Grivas and Puccio 2012).

Nurture good ideas

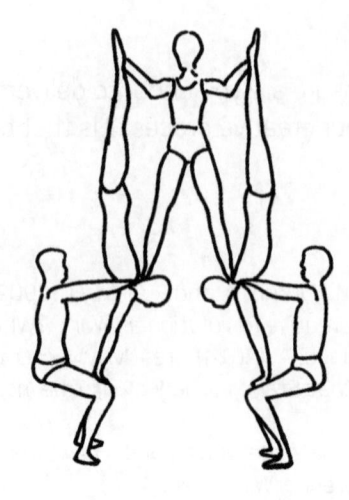

At Pixar, everyone developing a movie shares incomplete work at a series of daily meetings, where everyone is free to make suggestions. 'When the embarrassment goes away,' says founder Ed Catmull, 'people become more creative. By making the struggles to solve problems safe to discuss, everyone learns from and inspires one another' (Catmull and Wallace 2014).

Developing your idea might make you reconsider your original aims. However, according to psychologist Gary Klein, we often resist 'goal insights' because it feels like abandoning the work we've done up to that point. Klein argues that conflict and anxiety about goals could act as 'a divining rod that directs us to shaky assumptions we've been making' (Klein 2014).

How

1. Adopt the habits of Pixar's daily development meetings

Use this template to shape how you respond to someone else's ideas.

Big picture

Listen: don't just wait for a gap to jump in and add your thoughts. Properly listen to what people say. Make notes to help focus on their idea.	Empathy: understand how vulnerable someone feels sharing incomplete work. What could you say to support them?
	Generosity: you all want to make it work, not score points. How can you help?
	Clarity: critique the idea, not the person.

2. Respond to ideas with questions, not judgements or actions

What do people say when they judge new ideas or want to act on them too quickly? How you could turn those responses into open-ended questions?

Judgement/action response	Questioning response
X won't like this	How could we get X to support this?
It's too expensive	How could we justify the budget?
We've tried this already	
I don't get it	
We don't need this	
Write it up for me	
I need a cost/benefit analysis	
You've missed out X	
This won't work	
(add your own)	

3. Look out for goal insights and shaky assumptions

Are you having doubts about whether this is the right idea to develop after all? Are you having doubts about the overall aim of your project? Share these with the team. Watch for conflict or anxiety in the team. What shaky assumptions could it point towards?

Reflection

How does the conversation about ideas change when you respond with questions rather than judgement? Are you comfortable with having goal insights mid-way through your project?

References

Catmull, E. and Wallace, A. (2014) *Creativity, Inc. Overcoming the Unseen Forces that Stand in the Way of True Inspiration.* Bantam Press.

Grivas, C. and Puccio, G.J. (2012) *The Innovative Team: Unleashing Creative Potential for Breakthrough Results.* Jossey-Bass.

Klein, G. (2014) *Seeing What Others Don't: The Remarkable Ways We Gain Insights.* Nicholas Brealey Publishing.

5.3 Widen your pool of talent

Why

Several large companies, such as Nike, Roche and LEGO, embrace aspects of open innovation, sharing information or setting specific challenges with people from outside their organisation. Open-source innovation communities on the internet create highly successful new products and disrupt old business models.

There are problems associated with opening up your creative process: commercial confidentiality, intellectual property, reputation management to name just three. It would sound desperate if you started your creative process by asking, 'Anyone out there got any ideas?' But once you're certain of your mission and you've got some early ideas, you could make them stronger by carefully fishing in a wider pool of talent.

Knowledge briefing

The theory of the 'wisdom of the crowd' says diverse groups can outperform experts when it comes to complex tasks or problems (Surowiecki 2005; Page 2007).

This may be because they include 'naive experts' who know lots about your project, but from an outsider's point of view (Allan et al. 2002). Charles Leadbeater argues that the internet has created a new breed of 'pro-am producers'. These are passionate amateurs who take their unpaid work as seriously as any professional. They are highly connected and a source of disruptive new ideas and behaviours (Leadbeater 2005).

This can be unnerving for large organisations. When hackers published the code behind LEGO's first robotics kit, LEGO considered legal action. But the company chose instead to work with the online community and encourage experimentation. Mindstorms went on to become LEGO's best-selling single product ever. Its successor – Mindstorms NXT – was developed with the help of volunteer superfans. But LEGO decided NXT's key parameters in advance, managed a small clique of co-creators and always retained final sign-off. Despite the success of Mindstorms, LEGO still develop most of their products in secret (Robertson 2013).

Companies like Apple don't have open innovation. But inside that secretive organisation, Apple's researchers, designers, marketers and engineers work together on all stages of development, taking an open-within-our-closed-world approach (Johnson 2010).

How

1. Open up inside your organisation

How can you bring people into your creative process from other parts of the organisation? Could someone who deals with customer complaints help with idea generation? Could your idea developers sit and handle customer complaints for a day?

2. Open up to outsiders (but learn from LEGO)

See David Robertson's *Brick by Brick* (2013) for a more detailed account.

LEGO and open innovation	Open innovation and your project
What's the benefit? LEGO only opened up when they could see that outsiders had expertise they lacked.	Where could outsiders have more expertise than you?
Fixed direction, flexible execution. LEGO set all the major parameters in advance (e.g. budget, playability, target age range), but gave their volunteers leeway within those goals.	What are your fixed goals? Where do you have flexibility?
Be advocate and enforcer. LEGO execs had to champion their volunteers' ideas within a sceptical organisation and remind the fans that many of company's rules were fixed.	Which rules are non-negotiable? How could you advocate outsiders' ideas inside your organisation?
Low cost, low risk. LEGO found that the 'give it a try' ethos of the maker community allowed them to take a series of small, inexpensive risks ('minor investment points') to test new ideas.	What could your minor investment points be?

Reflection

How do you feel about opening up your creative process? What reaction would it get from those around you? How could you prove it's an experiment worth trying?

References

Allan, D., Kingdon, M., Murrin, K. and Rudkin, D. (2002) *Sticky Wisdom: How to Start a Creative Revolution at Work.* ?WhatIf! Publications.

Johnson, S. (2010) *Where Good Ideas Come From: The Natural History of Innovation.* Penguin Books.

Leadbeater, C. (2005) The era of open innovation. TED Talks.

Page, S.E. (2007) *The Difference: How the Power of Diversity Creates Better Groups, Firms, Schools and Societies.* Princeton University Press.

Robertson, D. (2013) *Brick by Brick: How LEGO Rewrote the Rules of Innovation.* Random House Business Books.

Surowiecki, J. (2005) *The Wisdom of Crowds: Why the Many Are Smarter than the Few and How Collective Wisdom Shapes Business, Economies, Societies and Nations.* First Anchor Books.

5.4 Design thinking

Why

If you think of design as something that happens after you've had an idea, to package it up nicely, then you may be missing a whole series of tricks. Good design is about problem-solving in a way that makes sense for consumers and producers. Good designers are everywhere, not just in design schools and agencies.

Design thinking is not just about making a product or service look good, it can fundamentally shape the idea behind it.

Many of the stages in this book could be described as design thinking: defining your problem (Chapter 2), seeking insights from the world of your project (Chapter 3) and brainstorming possibilities (Chapter 4).

Knowledge briefing

Design thinking means 'empathy with users, a discipline of prototyping, and tolerance for failure', according to product designer Jon Kolko. Think about design, he argues 'less as a way of making things look a certain way, and more as a way of getting things done' (Kolko 2014, 2015).

Google constantly run live tests for potential improvements to their services. In 2010, Google developers ran over 8,000 separate A/B tests on their search function alone. The company doesn't just tolerate failure, it actually rewards 'thoughtful failures', albeit not as lucratively as spectacular successes (Bock 2015).

The internet has driven communication, distribution and collaboration costs down so much that the cost of trying out a new thing has become 'nearly zero', according to Joi Ito at the MIT Media Lab. MIT's approach to new ideas used to be 'Demo or die', because a demo only needed to work once before business could be persuaded to develop it. Nowadays MIT's motto is 'Deploy or die'. MIT now believe that testing an idea by deploying it now in the real world is better than trying to plan for an increasingly unpredictable future. 'I don't like the word futurist,' says Ito. 'I think we should be now-ists' (Ito 2014).

How

1. What can you get out of your 'thoughtful failures'?

Insight	What assumptions did you make that turned out to be wrong?
Mission	What could these insights tell you about your wider mission?
Next time	What could you do differently?
Sharing	How could you ensure others don't make similar mistakes?

2. How can you be a now-ist?

What elements of your project can you try out in the real world right now? What could you learn from a road-test? What's the smallest, cheapest, fastest way of prototyping your project?

3. Evaluate results from your prototypes against your original aims

- Group or solo exercise, 40–60 minutes. You'll need sticky notes; worksheet optional.
- Write your original aims under *Target*.
- Write the results of your prototype tests as 'darts' on sticky notes. Use several different measures of performance.
- Arrange them based on how close they landed near the bullseye.

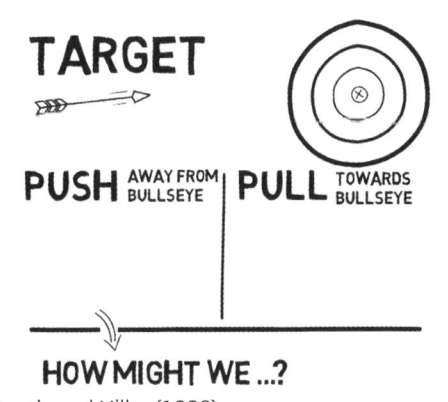

TARGET

PUSH AWAY FROM BULLSEYE | **PULL** TOWARDS BULLSEYE

HOW MIGHT WE ...?

Source: From Puccio and Miller (1996).

Nurture good ideas

- List what was pulling them closer to the target.
- List what was pushing them further away.
- Turn the push factors into 'How could we . . . ?' questions and use these to make the next prototype stronger. So, for example, if lack of senior management support was a push factor, you would ask, 'How could we make senior managers more enthusiastic about this project?'

Reflection

How do you feel about testing ideas and sharing the results with others, regardless of success or failure?

References

Bock, L. (2015) *Work Rules! Insights from Inside Google that Will Transform How You Live and Lead.* John Murray.

Ito, J. (2014) Want to innovate? Become a 'now-ist'. TED Talks.

Kolko, J. (2014) *Well Designed: How to Use Empathy to Create Products People Love.* Harvard Business Review Press.

Kolko, J. (2015) Design thinking comes of age, *Harvard Business Review,* September.

Puccio, G.J. and Miller, B. (1996) *Targeting: Tool for Evaluation and Group Consensus,* 42nd Annual Creative Problem Solving Institute, Buffalo, New York.

5.5 Keep the novelty alive

Why

The more we work in high-pressure environments, the more we're likely to react fast to a new idea. We measure the new against what we already know, judge it and accept or reject it straight away. Then we move on to the next new thing that has just landed in our inbox.

In this climate, novelty can seem frivolous or stupid. Even though we know we're meant to be innovating, we are sorely tempted to reject any idea that we can't immediately see a use for. It takes real effort to resist the pressure to deliver workable solutions right away. It's hard to keep the novelty alive.

Big picture

Knowledge briefing

Many of us have an *unconscious* bias against creativity, preferring to take the safe option when we feel uncertain about the outcome. This bias can exist even when we say we want creative ideas. Uncertainty about the future might be the trigger that starts us looking for new ideas, but ironically 'uncertainty also makes us less able to recognise creativity, perhaps when we need it most' (Mueller *et al.* 2011).

If we are feeling uncertain about a new idea, it is very easy to react to it by finding faults. 'Most of us tend to confuse critical thinking with criticism,' according to Roger Firestien. 'Critical thinking is carefully examining an idea to look at both its strengths and weaknesses, not just its shortcomings.' Always make time to look for the positives and potential in a new idea first, before moving on to your concerns. Phrase your concerns as questions that could lead to further new thinking, rather than as statements (Firestien 1996).

Psychologist Gary Klein suggests organisations where new ideas can be stifled by hierarchy could set up 'escape hatches'. These would allow junior staff to leapfrog resistant immediate superiors if they feel a valuable new idea is being unreasonably rejected (Klein 2014).

How

1. First, remind everyone why we're here

If you are genuinely looking for new ideas, then accepting more of the same from inside your comfort zone just isn't enough. Remind people – we're here to find novel ideas. It's going to feel uncomfortable at this stage and that's okay.

2. Respond to a new idea with pluses, potentials and concerns[10]

- Solo or group exercise, 30–40 minutes. You'll need copies of the worksheet.

Use this technique to give new ideas breathing space. When you hear a new idea:

- Pause, then find at least *one* positive thing to say about the idea: 'I like that idea because . . .'
- Find at least *one* potential spin-off: 'If we did this, we could also . . .'
- Raise your concerns as questions: 'How could we . . . ?'
- Turn those 'How could we . . . ?' questions into starting points to brainstorm solutions.

As a group exercise: take a new idea and put it through the PPC template. Ask everyone to come up with at least three positives, potentials and concerns. Turn the concerns into open-ended questions, then come up with as many ideas as possible for dealing with them.

---

[10] This technique is from Firestien (1996).

PLUSES POTENTIALS CONCERNS

WHAT'S YOUR IDEA?

FIND AT LEAST THREE PLUSES OR POSITIVES	'I LIKE YOUR IDEA BECAUSE...'

FIND AT LEAST THREE POTENTIAL SPIN-OFFS	'IT COULD ALSO...'

PLUSES POTENTIALS CONCERNS

WHAT'S YOUR IDEA?

FIND AT LEAST THREE CONCERNS	PHRASED AS 'HOW MIGHT WE...?' QUESTIONS

NEW IDEAS FOR OVERCOMING CONCERNS	

Source: Based on Firestien (1996).

3. Set up escape hatches for novel ideas

What happens to new ideas that are rejected in your workplace? Is there a way to get a second opinion without upsetting corporate egos? This could be as simple as a humble suggestions box. Maybe you could have an explicit rule that it's okay to discuss your idea with someone else, even if your immediate superior didn't go for it – see the Pixar rule (Section 3.3).

Reflection

What difference does it make when you react to new ideas using PPC? How easy is it to turn your concerns into open-ended questions? How do people around you react when you take this approach?

References

Firestien, R. (1996) *Leading on the Creative Edge: Gaining Competitive Advantage through the Power of Creative Problem Solving.* Pinon Press.

Klein, G. (2014) *Seeing What Others Don't: The Remarkable Ways We Gain Insights.* Nicholas Brealey Publishing.

Mueller, J.S., Melwani, S. and Goncalo, J.A. (2011) *The Bias Against Creativity: Why People Desire But Reject Creative Ideas.* Cornell University ILR School.

5.6 Working with wild ideas

Why

If you really throw yourself into the creative process, there's bound to come a point when you look at an idea, and think 'this is crazy'. It's most likely when you're being ambitious and trying for fundamental change rather than incremental improvement. Or when you're working with people who don't see the world the same way you do.

Sometimes you have to fight to keep the wild idea alive. Sometimes you will have to move to a more practical solution. But how can you do that without killing the excitement and energy you've developed so far? How can you turn 'this is crazy' into 'there might be something in this . . .'?

Knowledge briefing

The founder of brainstorming, Alex Osborn, once said, 'It's easier to tame down a wild idea than it is to invigorate a weak one.'

By association, a wild idea could help you make a link to more workable ideas. These could be original solutions which you'd never have found if you'd immediately dismissed the first wild idea (Osborn 1948).

When the US Patent Office decide whether to grant a patent on a new invention, they consider if it's new and useful but also non-obvious: in other words, surprising. According to Dean Keith Simonton, creativity is at its best when it produces functional, new and unexpected ideas (Kersting 2003).

What seems to you to be a wild and impractical idea might appeal to the people you're trying to reach. Decision-makers within businesses prefer feasible and profitable ideas while their customers value novelty, rarity and creativity. If you switch from a 'how do we do this?' to a 'why are we doing this?' mindset, it might allow you to be more tolerant of uncertainty and happier to consider wild ideas (Mueller 2014).

How

1. Go to the heart of the wild idea

- Group or solo exercise, 30–40 minutes. Worksheet optional.

When you've come up with an idea that everyone likes but is just too wild to take forward, use it as a spark to find another idea.

Nurture good ideas

THE HEART OF A WILD IDEA

(diagram of a heart with numbered list 1–5 inside labelled "LIST ALL THE REASONS WHY WE LOVE THE WILD IDEA", and rays extending outward numbered 1–5 labelled "HOW COULD WE ACHIEVE THIS QUALITY WITHIN OUR CONSTRAINTS?")

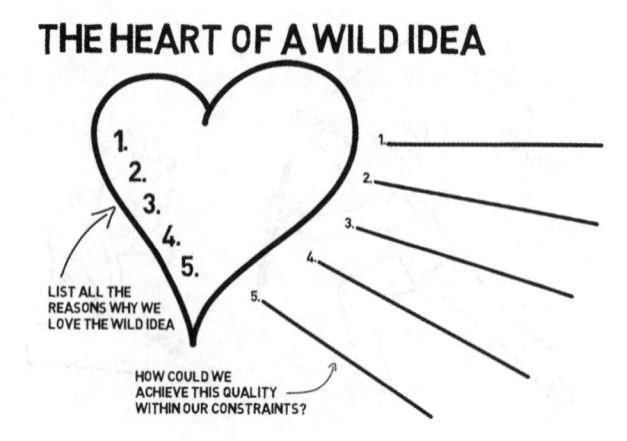

- Ask 'why do we all like this idea?' Go for lots of qualities.
- Take the first on the list and ask 'how can we achieve this quality within our constraints?'
- Write down lots of ideas then move on to the next quality and repeat the process.
- Review the ideas that have emerged. Which ones are new? Which ones still contain some of the excitement of the original wild idea? Which ones are more practical?

2. Is the idea really that wild?

- Group or solo exercise, 30–40 minutes.

Switch from 'how?' to 'why?' then see how you feel. The people your project is aimed at – your customers or audience – don't care *how* you make it work, they only care *why* they might want to use it.

Take the 'wild' idea and spend 10 minutes listing all the reasons why you might want to do it and why your customers might love it.

Forget *how* you're going to do this for now and focus instead on:	
Why we might want to do it . . .	Why our customers might love it . . .

Big picture

3. Are we having FUN yet?

- Group exercise, 30–40 minutes, longer if you are comparing a number of ideas. You'll need sticky notes, flip chart, one worksheet per person.

Ask people to score the new idea you're considering by how far it is: Functional; Unexpected; New.

HAVING FUN YET?

SCORE OUT OF 10

FUNCTIONAL
- DOES IT WORK?
- DOES IT SOLVE OUR ORIGINAL PROBLEM?

UNEXPECTED
- IS IT A SURPRISING SOLUTION?
- IS IT SIMILAR TO OTHER IDEAS?

NEW
- HOW NOVEL IS THIS IDEA?
- HAS IT BEEN DONE BEFORE?

This should be done silently on separate worksheets so people don't influence one another's opinions. Now use sticky notes to compare their scores on a flip chart.

Clusters of sticky notes indicate consensus; a wide spread of scores indicates disagreement within the team, which is worth exploring.

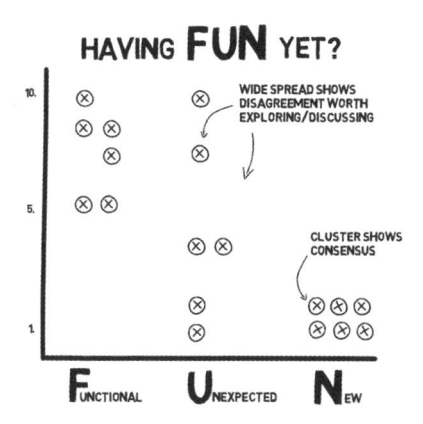

HAVING FUN YET?

WIDE SPREAD SHOWS DISAGREEMENT WORTH EXPLORING/DISCUSSING

CLUSTER SHOWS CONSENSUS

FUNCTIONAL   **U**NEXPECTED   **N**EW

If you need to tame a bunch of wild ideas, look for those which score highest on Functional. If you want to keep the novelty alive, then you should be choosing ideas which score high on Unexpected and New.

Reflection

How tempted are you to stick with functional ideas rather than take a risk on novelty?

References

Kersting, K. (2003) What exactly is creativity? Psychologists continue their quest to better understand creativity, *American Psychological Association,* 34(10).

Mueller, J. (2014) Managers reject ideas customers want, *Harvard Business Review,* July–August.

Osborn, A. (1948) *Your Creative Power.* Scribner.

5.7 Move out of the greenhouse

Why

You've tested your idea, you've tried out the prototype and now your time in the greenhouse is up. Take your seedling idea and plant it out. Or, if it isn't good enough, throw it out.

At this stage, you need to figure out where your new idea stands in relation to everything else that's going on around you. Have you got a radical, game-changing idea or a clever twist on something that's already happening? What does this mean when you come to sell your idea to the people who will put it into action?

If you have to reject an idea at the end of the development period, it's important to say why. If you seem to be saying no on a whim or a hunch, this sends out confusing signals and suggests you're not thinking about your project goals clearly.

Knowledge briefing

We shouldn't underestimate the time and effort needed to carry through truly innovative ideas.

LEGO tried to pull off a number of simultaneous 'never seen before' innovations to redefine their place in the toy market during the early 2000s. Complexity mushroomed in the organisation, costs rose and profits fell to the point where LEGO faced bankruptcy. As they rebuilt their company, LEGO recognised the different demands that readjusting, reconfiguring or redefining their toys would put on the company (Robertson 2013).

Other people are more likely to support your innovation if they can see its value. Everett M. Rogers identified five factors which led to rapid adoption of new ideas: relative advantage, compatibility, complexity, trialability and observability (Rogers 2003).

You must set a clear direction for anyone working with you on your project, right from the start and right up to the point that you say no to an idea. 'People must understand the reason for the no,' according to Roger Firestien, 'then they will come back with other ideas that could help' (Firestien 1996).

How

1. Use the LEGO innovation matrix[11]

- Group or solo exercise, 40–60 minutes. You'll need copies of the worksheet.

This technique is useful if you have a number of ideas and need to decide which ones to make your priority, or if you want your new idea to exploit a full spectrum of innovation. The more ambitious your innovation, the greater the demands on your organisation.

- *Adjust:* tweaking what you've got to freshen it up. This is a low-risk and low-cost option. In LEGO terms, this is like creating LEGO Harry Potter based on the success of LEGO Star Wars. These can be 'small but very profitable' innovations.
- *Reconfigure:* coming up with new combinations of ideas within an existing category. For LEGO, think of the Bionicle: it used a skeleton structure but was still a toy you build and play with. These innovations 'change the terms of competition in an existing market'.
- *Redefine category:* changing the game and carving out a new market. LEGO Universe tried to create an online brick-building platform, but they were too slow and Minecraft beat them to it. These are 'the most difficult and disruptive innovations' to pull off.

LEGO also identified four categories for innovation, which make up the vertical axis of the matrix: *Product*, *Business*, *Communication* and *Process*.

Arrange your ideas on the matrix. Do your new ideas innovate in more than one category? What else could you do to achieve a full spectrum of innovation right across the vertical axis? Are you attempting too many disruptive innovations at the same time?

---

[11] This technique is from Robertson (2013).

Big picture

LEGO INNOVATION MATRIX

ADJUST
LOW-RISK TWEAKS

RECONFIGURE
NEW IDEAS IN
EXISTING CATEGORY

REDEFINE
HIGH RISK
GAME-CHANGING

PRODUCT   BUSINESS   COMMUNICATION   PROCESS

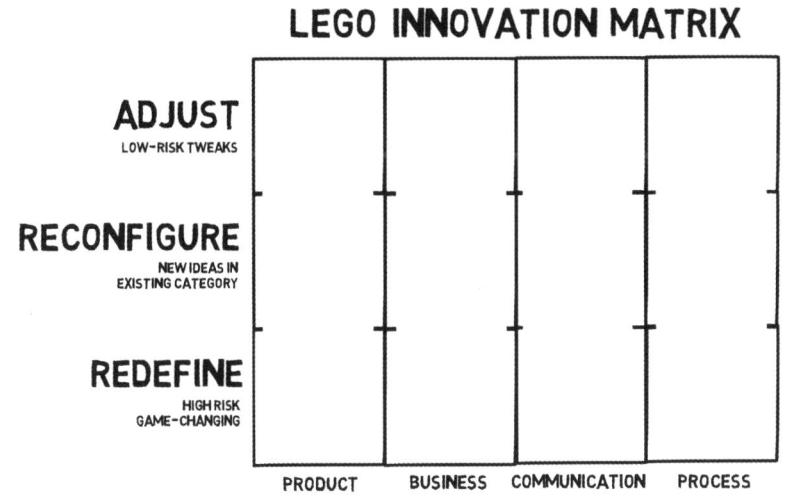

Source: Based on Robertson (2013).

2. Use Everett Rogers' innovation checklist

- Group or solo exercise, 30–40 minutes.

If you want your seedling to thrive in its new environment, see how it scores on this checklist before letting it out of the greenhouse.

Everett Rogers' innovation checklist	
Relative advantage	How does your idea offer a better solution than what people are using already? How can you show it's got an edge on its competitors?
Compatibility	How far does your idea fit with people's values and beliefs? How close is it to what they need or already understand?
Complexity	How hard is it to understand? How can you make it seem less complex?
Trialability	How easy is it for your customers to take a low-risk test drive?
Observability	How easy is it for them to see other people adopting your idea?

Nurture good ideas

> **Tip**
>
> Use the Rogers checklist or the FUN scale (Section 5.6) to make it clear why you are saying no to those ideas that don't make it out of the greenhouse.

Reflection

How does this development process compare to what normally happens in your workplace? How much appetite is there in your organisation for disruptive game-changing innovation? What advantages can you see in setting out your reasons for rejecting an idea?

References

Firestien, R. (1996) *Leading on the Creative Edge: Gaining Competitive Advantage through the Power of Creative Problem Solving*. Pinon Press.

Robertson, D. (2013) *Brick by Brick: How LEGO Rewrote the Rules of Innovation and Conquered the Global Toy Industry*. Random House Business Books.

Rogers, E.M. (2003) *Diffusion of Innovations*. 5th edition. Simon & Schuster.

Simonton, D.K. (2013) Creativity in science, in Fesit, G. and Gorman, M., *Handbook of the Psychology of Science*. Springer Publishing Company.

Chapter 6

Weed out bad ideas

- **6.1** Get serious
- **6.2** The unknown
- **6.3** Groupthink
- **6.4** Optimism bias
- **6.5** Overconfidence
- **6.6** The sunk cost fallacy (aka why it's hard to pull the plug)
- **6.7** How to fail well

SPEED READ
6. Weed out bad ideas

6.1 Get serious

Spotting bad ideas is a serious business. That's not to say that the creative process up to now has been frivolous – after all, you've dedicated time and effort to get this far. But however uncomfortable you might find it, it's better to look hard for mistakes now, before committing to action.

We all get wedded to our own ideas, especially once we've put a lot of work into them. We accentuate the positive when we have to sell the idea to others. But the positive, optimistic and good-humoured attitude that encourages new ideas might stop you spotting bad ones. So it's time to get serious.

Often the knowledge required to spot and deal with bad ideas lies within you or your team, waiting for a chance to surface. The techniques in this chapter give the nagging voice of doubt permission to speak.

Weed out bad ideas

> **Do this**
> Think about how you go about finding weaknesses in your own ideas before committing to action. How ready are you to find flaws in your own ideas?

6.2 The unknown

However much we think we know, there's always more we don't. Fear of the unknown stops people taking action, exploring or pushing for change. You can't come up with brave new ideas without taking a step into the unknown.

We have a remarkable ability to focus on what's in front of us, ignoring what we can't see, to the extent that we even forget it might exist.

We use mental shortcuts to deal with vast amounts of information quickly. These biases are like blinkers on a horse, allowing us to work fast.

This is all very well, until we are hit by something from our blind side.

> **Do this**
> Consider how much you know about your project. Are you confident that you have all the essential information or are you happy to work with a partial picture? When have you been caught out in the past by unknown information?

6.3 Groupthink

Any group of people that works together for a long time can start to think alike. Unwritten rules shape how the group works and what kinds of ideas it upholds. We have natural tendencies to seek harmony in social groups.

But when this becomes groupthink, we create an environment that allows errors to flourish unchecked. Groupthink creates teams where outsiders find it hard to be heard and where looming problems can't be discussed openly. This can come from autocratic leaders who don't tolerate dissent. It can also come from willing-to-please subordinates who think group harmony is the priority.

Do this
Have you worked in a group with a very strong identity and culture, where people could second-guess each other? How did that group react to bad news, criticism or failure?

6.4 Optimism bias

Optimism sounds like a blessing: the ability to see a glass half full. Entrepreneurs are optimistic about their new business ventures. Newly married couples are optimistic about their chances of a long and happy life together. We sign expensive gym

HALF FULL

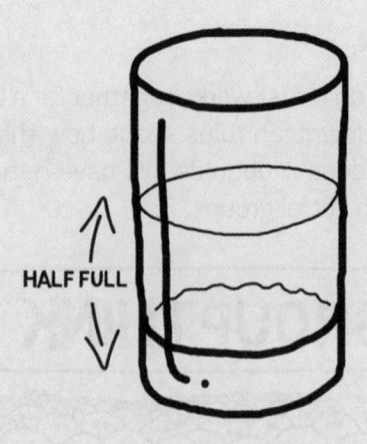

memberships in early January, imagining we'll have a beach body by the summer. But businesses fail, marriages end in divorce and gym memberships lie unused, despite our best intentions.

This is not to say we should all become pessimists. After all, if it wasn't for optimism, we'd never start anything new or demanding. But we need to be aware we may have a bias towards optimism that needs reining in at crucial moments. When the stakes are high, it's foolish not to plan for worst case scenarios too.

Do this
Think about what has made you optimistic in the past. Has that optimism always been justified by events?

6.5 Overconfidence

Confidence is attractive. We are drawn towards confident people and often wish we could be more confident ourselves, especially in work. But how can you tell the difference between justified confidence, based on ability, and overconfidence? On the surface they look remarkably similar.

Speed read

This is another area where our mental shortcuts play a part. If you like a neat picture with all the loose ends tied up, if you like an expert with strong views on what's going to happen next, if you like to think the world makes sense, this may be more to do with your cognitive biases than what's really going on. But when the stakes are high it's good to try a more sceptical approach.

Do this

Think about the most confident statements you've heard or made about work in the past. How many of them turned out to be accurate?

6.6 The sunk cost fallacy (aka why it's hard to pull the plug)

Nobody likes to lose time, money or reputation by getting something wrong. Ironically, this loss aversion can backfire, causing us to throw good money after bad when things start to drift off course. The pressure of dealing with a project that's sinking fast can blind us to the need for drastic action.

Weed out bad ideas

It's easy to talk about cutting your losses, but the size of those losses can dominate your thinking. Sometimes the simple act of reframing losses as lessons can help you regain focus on what needs to be done next.

> **Do this**
> Think back to the last time you gave up on something you had put a lot of time and effort into, whether at work or in your personal life. How did that loss feel at the time and afterwards? How far would you go to avoid these feelings?

6.7 How to fail well

You're bound to fail at some point in the creative process. What matters is how you come back from failure. Unless you're an air traffic controller or a brain surgeon, there's no point screwing down every possible source of error. There just isn't enough time in the day, plus it's a joyless exercise. It's not about insisting nothing can ever be allowed to go wrong; it's about realising something will inevitably go wrong and making sure you've got the resilience to cope.

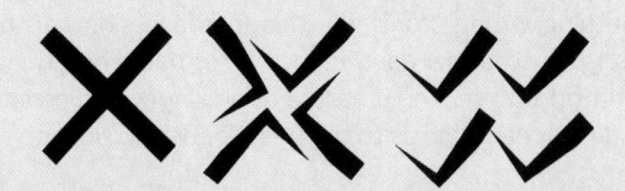

In fact, without error there'd be nothing new. Evolution moves forwards thanks only to genetic errors. Plenty of new ideas came from mistakes – the discovery of penicillin and sticky notes, for example. Nobody likes to fail. But you're going to fail at some point, so you might as well get the most out of it.

Do this
Consider your attitude to failure. How does it make you feel? What about other people around you? Do you know anyone who discusses their own failures in terms of what lessons they learned?

BIG PICTURE
6. Weed out bad ideas

6.1 Get serious

Why

You need to approach most stages of the creative process with a playful attitude. If you want lots of new ideas, you need to tolerate ambiguity and even error. You suspend your judgement and see where the flow of ideas might take you. A wrong idea might spark a better idea; a faulty assumption can lead to an insight.

Imagination needs a playful mind, but evaluation does not. We can toy with ideas, we can play with possibilities, but we have to get serious when it comes to errors. Getting serious doesn't mean getting bitter, solemn or harshly critical. You still need to pay attention to group dynamics and emotional undercurrents.

Knowledge briefing

A good mood increases our sense of 'cognitive ease', meaning that our thinking feels not just effortless but also true. But this also increases the risk of bias. 'When in a good mood, people become more intuitive and more creative but also less vigilant and more prone to logical errors,' according to psychologist Daniel Kahneman. 'At the other pole, sadness, vigilance, suspicion [and] an analytic approach' are all connected with increased cognitive effort. In other words, this is when we are thinking harder (Kahneman 2011).

Silence, patience, doubt and humility are 'negative capabilities' we should employ when we are working up to the edge of our knowledge. These qualities allow us to stop pretending we know everything. They encourage others to help us explore areas we aren't sure about and point out errors we might have missed (D'Souza and Renner 2015).

What we think of as negative emotions, such as sadness and fear, have an important part to play in our thinking. Sadness can sap our energy but at the same time 'focuses the mind to seek a happier situation', according to Charles Burnette. Fear makes us analyse a situation, prepare for action and plan how to avoid hazards in the future (Burnette 2009).

How

1. Set your risk thermostat

Imagine a sliding scale of tolerable risk, with poetry at one end and air traffic control at the other. Work out where you are on this scale with your project and share this with your team. This can send an important signal about how much error you are happy to tolerate at this stage in your project.

This will change over time: your tolerance of error should be pretty low by the time you hit 'Send' on your pre-launch press release.

Big picture

YOUR RISK THERMOSTAT

MIN — MAX

LOW-RISK TOLERANCE ⇔ HIGH-RISK TOLERANCE

BRAIN SURGEON
AIR TRAFFIC CONTROLLER

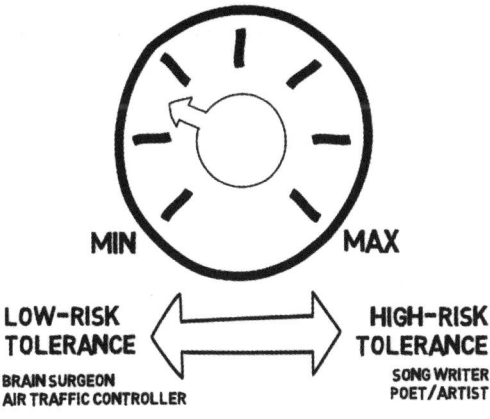

SONG WRITER
POET/ARTIST

WHERE ARE WE NOW? HOW COULD THAT CHANGE OVER TIME?

2. Plot problems on a matrix

A matrix can help you converge on the most important problem. See two examples below of how you can plot problems on a matrix:

Serious vs likely

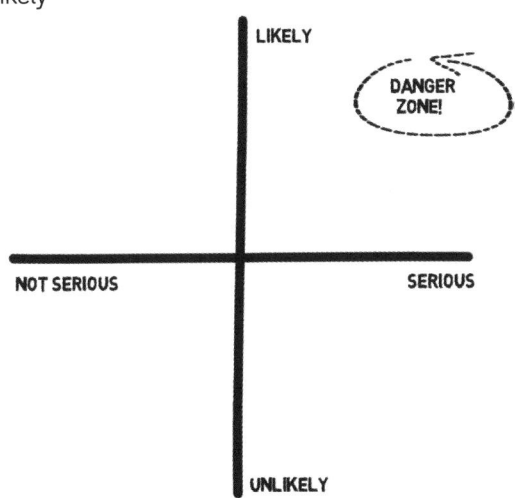

LIKELY

DANGER ZONE!

NOT SERIOUS — SERIOUS

UNLIKELY

Weed out bad ideas

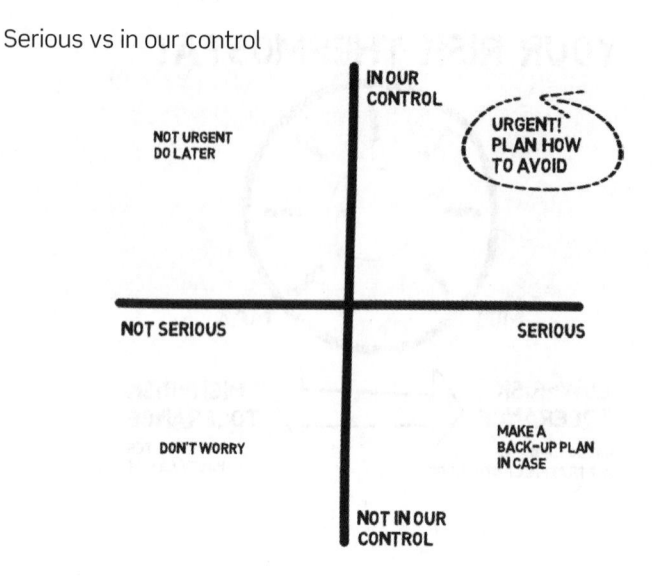

Serious vs in our control

```
                    IN OUR
                    CONTROL
        NOT URGENT              URGENT!
        DO LATER                PLAN HOW
                                TO AVOID


    NOT SERIOUS         |         SERIOUS
    ————————————————————+————————————————————


        DON'T WORRY             MAKE A
                                BACK-UP PLAN
                                IN CASE
                    NOT IN OUR
                    CONTROL
```

3. Signal the change of mood

How can you make it clear to others that you need to move from a playful attitude to a serious one, without turning your next session into a battleground? Establish ground rules based on D'Souza and Renner's (2015) negative capabilities:

- *Silence:* we will listen fully to ideas before jumping in with our own thoughts.
- *Patience:* this process will take time, there's no rush to judgement.
- *Doubt:* we are trying to do something new, it's okay to voice doubts.
- *Humility:* not one of us has all the answers, we are here to help each other.

4. Find 99 problems

- Group or solo exercise, 15–20 minutes.

This divergent technique is adapted from Luciano Passuello's 'List of 100' technique (with a nod to Jay-Z). If you are in a group, get everyone to do it solo first then compare notes.

Write a list of 99 problems that your project could face. This seems like a huge task, but persevere. If you have lingering doubts about your project, they will come out in the first 30. The next 40 will show any patterns. The last 29 will bring out unusual combinations and could contain real gems.

When you've completed your list, go back through it and highlight any problems worth further action. Turn these into 'How could we . . .?' questions to brainstorm.

> **Tip**
> Don't worry that deliberately looking for problems will dishearten you. Ironically, the harder we have to search for evidence of something, the less likely we are to believe it. If I asked you to find just two problems that would be so easy you'd suspect there must be more out there (see Daniel Kahneman's [2011] book for an explanation of this 'availability heuristic').

5. Just give me a sign!

- Group exercise, 30–40 minutes. Download photocards showing warning signs (from www.newthinking.tools) or use road signs from the Highway Code.

This lateral thinking technique mirrors the lateral nudge technique (Section 3.2) and is designed to bring lingering or non-obvious doubts to the surface.

- Ask everyone to spend up to 10 minutes writing down all the obvious problems they can think of that might affect your project.
- Now give everyone a card each with an image of a warning sign. These can be handed out at random – there is no 'correct' warning.
- Ask people to think of any ways that warning could relate to your project. At this point, it helps to have an example ready (see below).

Weed out bad ideas

JUST GIVE ME A SIGN!

- who's going to clean up any mess?
- are we being anti-social?
- are we on shaky ground?
- is there trouble coming from above?
- are we being too pedestrian?
- does someone need their hand holding?

- Encourage them to go for lots of problems at first, without going into detail on any one of them. Encourage lateral thinking – interpret the signs as widely as possible.
- If people exhaust the potential problems from one sign, give them another.
- With 10 minutes to go, ask people to look back over the first list made and any additional problems that have surfaced from the signs exercise.
- Choose which problems are worth investigating further.

Turn any outstanding problems into 'How could we . . .?' questions to brainstorm or assign people to work on them.

Reflection

How hard do you find it to set a serious mood without getting solemn or negative? How do you feel about embracing doubt? What about others around you?

References

Burnette, C. (2009) An emotional basis for design thinking: http://www.academia.edu/251044/An_Emotional_Basis_for_Design_Thinking

D'Souza, S. and Renner, D. (2015) *Not Knowing: The Art of Turning Uncertainty into Opportunity*. LID Publishing.
Kahneman, D. (2011) *Thinking, Fast and Slow*. Penguin Books.
Passuello, L. (n.d.) Tackle any issue with a List of 100: https://litemind.com/tackle-any-issue-with-a-list-of-100/

6.2 The unknown

Why

Asked why the US hadn't found any weapons of mass destruction in Iraq, US Secretary of Defense Donald Rumsfeld gave what became famous as a classic politician's answer:

> 'There are known knowns. These are things we know that we know. There are known unknowns . . . things that we know we don't know. But there are also unknown unknowns. There are things we don't know we don't know.'

Politics aside, Rumsfeld was, of course, right. There are things we don't know we don't know, things we can't predict or even imagine, no matter how hard we try. These unknowns can completely derail what we're trying to achieve.

In complex and uncertain situations we will find ourselves facing the unknown. It is hard to make plans without making assumptions. The difficulty is knowing which assumptions are safe to accept and which need to be challenged.

Knowledge briefing

We have evolved to make rapid decisions based on what we can see right in front of us or vividly call to mind. When evidence is scarce, we are happy to jump to a conclusion. We are vaguely aware of gaps in our knowledge, but have no way of knowing how big they are. 'Our comforting conviction that the world makes sense rests on a secure foundation,' says psychologist Daniel Kahneman: 'our almost unlimited ability to ignore our own ignorance' (Kahneman 2011).

Military planners use 'what if?' analysis when looking ahead into an unknown future. This technique imagines a series of failed outcomes, tracks backwards to find plausible causes then generates warning signs that might indicate when a project is getting into trouble (University of Foreign Military and Cultural Studies 2012).

Nassim Nicholas Taleb, author of *The Black Swan*, is highly critical of the economists who trust abstract theories to deal with unknowable, unpredictable and highly disruptive events. 'For psychological comfort,' writes Taleb, 'some people would rather use a map of the Pyrenees while lost in the Alps than use nothing at all' (Taleb 2010).

Joi Ito at the MIT Lab also uses the metaphor of useless maps to describe how hard it is to plan in an increasingly complex world. His advice: rely on a compass, not maps. Don't try and map the entire territory, set a clear direction of travel and adapt to changing conditions as your journey unfolds (Ito 2014).

Pushing past the edge of what we know can be a liberating adventure, with as much surprise and excitement as doubt, according to Steven D'Souza and Diana Renner, authors of *Not Knowing*. We should adopt a 'beginner's mind' to embrace the creative potential of the unknown, because 'for the beginner, there are many possibilities, but for the expert there are few' (D'Souza and Renner 2015).

Big picture

How

1. Carry out a 'what if?' analysis[12]

- Group or solo exercise, 30–40 minutes.

For this exercise:

- Sketch out an ideal timeline for your project, complete with critical stages.
- Ask the group to suggest a series of 'what if?' alternative outcomes which would mean the project had failed.
- Think backwards to find plausible pathways to these 'what if?' outcomes. Look for lots of pathways and causes.
- With 10 minutes to go, choose the most serious and likely causes. Generate a list of indicators or warning signs that would tell you your project was about to drift off course.
- Keep the document and monitor those indicators as your project unfolds.

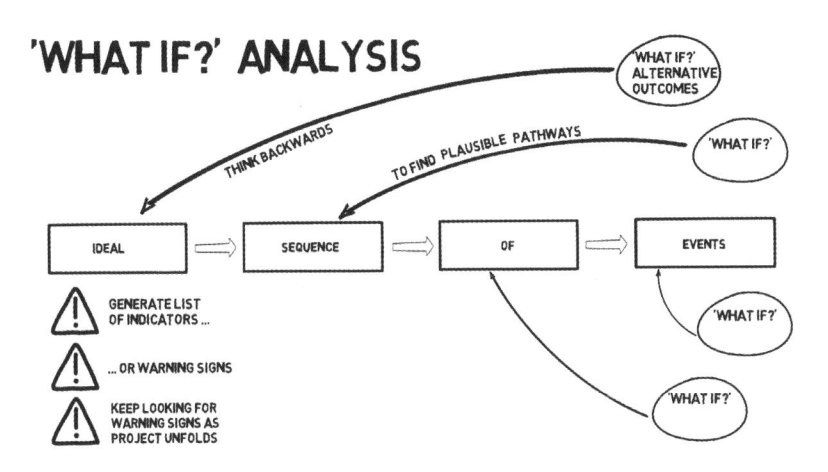

'WHAT IF?' ANALYSIS

```
                                            ┌──────────────┐
                                            │ WHAT IF?     │
                                            │ ALTERNATIVE  │
                                            │ OUTCOMES     │
                                            └──────────────┘
              THINK BACKWARDS
                    TO FIND PLAUSIBLE PATHWAYS       'WHAT IF?'

    ┌───────┐    ┌──────────┐    ┌────┐    ┌────────┐
    │ IDEAL │ ⇨  │ SEQUENCE │ ⇨  │ OF │ ⇨  │ EVENTS │
    └───────┘    └──────────┘    └────┘    └────────┘
                                                        'WHAT IF?'
    ⚠ GENERATE LIST
      OF INDICATORS...
    ⚠ ...OR WARNING SIGNS                               'WHAT IF?'
    ⚠ KEEP LOOKING FOR
      WARNING SIGNS AS
      PROJECT UNFOLDS
```

(The example on page 198 shows how you might use a 'what if?' analysis to generate warning signs for a project to introduce a new workplace training scheme.)

---

[12] This exercise is adapted from University of Foreign Military and Cultural Studies (2012).

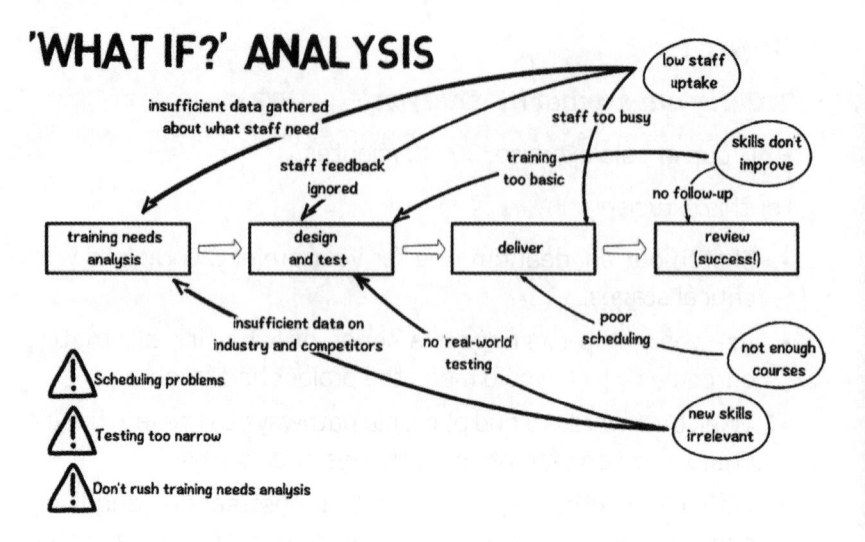

Weed out bad ideas

'WHAT IF?' ANALYSIS

Diagram: Flow from "training needs analysis" → "design and test" → "deliver" → "review (success!)" with what-if scenarios:
- insufficient data gathered about what staff need
- staff feedback ignored
- training too basic
- staff too busy
- low staff uptake
- skills don't improve
- no follow-up
- insufficient data on industry and competitors
- no real-world testing
- poor scheduling
- not enough courses
- new skills irrelevant

⚠ Scheduling problems
⚠ Testing too narrow
⚠ Don't rush training needs analysis

Source: Based on University of Foreign Military and Cultural Studies (2012).

2. Use a compass, not maps

- Group or solo exercise, 30–40 minutes.

Try the exercise in Section 2.1 to work out your project's direction of travel.

3. Adopt a beginner's mind (adopt a beginner)

- Group or solo exercise, 30–40 minutes.

It's hard to clear your head of everything you know about your project and approach it with a beginner's mind. So borrow a real beginner instead, such as a teenager, a student or an apprentice. Try to explain your project to someone who doesn't have all your intellectual baggage. Don't ask them to pretend to be experts. You want their genuine views and questions. If your project doesn't make sense to a beginner, perhaps your thinking isn't clear enough.

Reflection

How do these techniques make you feel now about the unknown? Daunted or excited? Are you happy to start a project if you still have gaps in your knowledge?

References

D'Souza, S. and Renner, D. (2015) *Not Knowing: The Art of Turning Uncertainty into Opportunity.* LID Publishing.
Ito, J. (2014) Want to innovate? Become a 'now-ist'. TED Talks.
Kahneman, D. (2011) *Thinking, Fast and Slow.* Penguin Books.
Taleb, N.N. (2010) *The Black Swan: The Impact of the Highly Improbable.* Penguin Books.
University of Foreign Military and Cultural Studies (2012) *Red Team Handbook.* UFMCS.

6.3 Groupthink

Why

Humans are social animals who experience strong pressures to conform. We can be insecure about our status and draw comfort from knowing that we see the world in the same way as others around us. When we work in groups, conformity can creep in without us even realising.

Knowledge briefing

The term 'groupthink' came from Irving Janis' study of how the Kennedy administration came so close to war over the Cuban missile crisis in 1962. Janis found that this like-minded group became over-optimistic about its decisions and allowed few dissenting voices to be heard. Pursuing consensus at any cost, individuals censored themselves, while self-appointed 'mind-guards' kept awkward information away from the group (Janis 2002).

Weed out bad ideas

GROUPTHINK

Groupthink is described by military theorists as one of the factors behind poor planning and operational mistakes. The US military suggests devil's advocacy as one way of combating groupthink (University of Foreign Military and Cultural Studies 2012).

We all have mental models which explain how the world works. When we work in groups, our individual models become part of a much more complex group model. 'As more people are added to any group,' says Ed Catmull, the founder of Pixar, 'there is an inexorable drift towards inflexibility' (Catmull and Wallace 2014).

How

1. Look for the warning signs of groupthink

Use this checklist adapted from Irving Janis' *Victims of Groupthink* (2002) to spot if your group is becoming conformist.

Big picture

Watch out for signs of:	If people say or think:
Illusion of invulnerability	'This can't fail' 'This has got to be right'
Inherent morality of the group	'We're doing the right thing' 'Outsiders are wrong/crazy/bad'
Censorship or self-censorship	'You can't say that' 'I shouldn't say that'
Illusion of unanimity	'We all think . . .' 'Everyone knows . . .'
Self-appointed 'mind-guards'	'The rest of the group don't need to know this'

2. Lead an open-minded group

How could you adapt these behaviours, recommended by Irving Janis, for your next discussion?

Accept criticism	How do you show that you can be influenced by those who disagree with you?
Hold back your views	Can you start a discussion without revealing your existing preferences or expectations?
Split the group	How could subgroups work on rival options before comparing and finding the strongest?
Outside voices	How can you bring alternative views into the group?
Alternative hypotheses	How can the group find alternative explanations for the situation they're considering? (See Section 6.2.)
Second chance	Is there a way for group members to voice concerns after a decision has been taken?

3. Play devil's advocate

Appoint one person to play devil's advocate in a discussion. Their job is to find all the reasons *not* to agree with the group. The devil's advocate should be told that the rest of the group:

- are inclined to believe first, then find evidence to confirm their beliefs

- tend to perceive what they expect to perceive
- overlook information that doesn't fit
- easily get wedded to their stated positions.

Ask the devil's advocate to prove the opposite of what the group thinks, either by:

- drawing different conclusions from the same evidence, or
- finding overlooked evidence.

Rotate the job of devil's advocate on a regular basis.

Reflection

How does the group you work with measure up to the groupthink test? Are you doing anything that reinforces this attitude? How do you feel about appointing a devil's advocate to knock down your arguments?

References

Catmull, E. and Wallace, A. (2014) *Creativity, Inc. Overcoming the Unseen Forces that Stand in the Way of True Inspiration.* Bantam Press.

Janis, I. (2002) *Victims of Groupthink: A Psychological Study of Foreign-Policy Decisions and Fiascoes.* Wadsworth.

University of Foreign Military and Cultural Studies (2012) *Red Team Handbook.* UFMCS.

6.4 Optimism bias

Why

Optimism is an attractive trait but it can mislead us. Ask anyone to rate their own abilities compared to others (for example, whether we are careful drivers or have a good sense of humour), and you'll find *the majority of us think we are above average.* It's a statistically impossible but fairly harmless delusion. Harmless, that is, until we start making serious decisions based on an optimistic outlook.

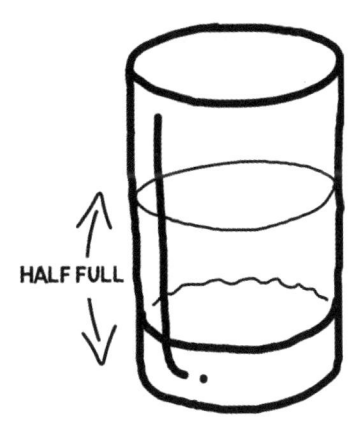

Smokers typically underestimate the risk that they will develop cancer; entrepreneurs underplay the risk of their business failing.

Once you've spent time and effort getting your project this far, you too will feel good about your chances of success. That's great, you'll need optimism to keep you going during the difficult times. As Nobel-Prize-winning psychologist Daniel Kahneman (2011) says, 'When action is needed, optimism, even of the mildly delusional variety, may be a good thing.'

So let's stay on the mildly delusional side of optimistic. But do a sense check before committing too heavily to your project. Is that glass really half full, or do you just prefer to see it that way?

Knowledge briefing

'Unrealistic optimism is a pervasive feature of human life,' according to social scientists Richard Thaler and Cass Sunstein. This can have a profound impact on our attitude to risk. If we are optimistic, it can stop us taking sensible preventative steps to avoid mistakes (Thaler and Sunstein 2009).

US military theorists recommend a pre-mortem analysis as a way of reducing optimism bias during the planning stage of military operations. Pre-mortems were developed by psychologist Dr Gary Klein as a way of questioning assumptions by imagining only worst-case scenarios. As the name suggests, this is a post-mortem that happens *before* anything has failed (Klein 1998; University of Foreign Military and Cultural Studies 2012).

Optimism about our own abilities often goes hand in hand with blindness to what normally happens in situations similar to our own. This explains why so many forecasts and cost estimates turn out to be inaccurate, according to Daniel Kahneman and Amos Tversky. They coined the term 'planning fallacy' to describe plans which are 'unrealistically close to best case scenarios [and] could be improved by consulting the statistics of similar cases'. Exploring worst-case scenarios and outsider views can help reduce optimism bias (Kahneman 2011).

You can reduce your own planning fallacy by benchmarking your project estimates against other similar cases. If you're planning to launch a new workplace training programme, for example, what does it cost to do this in similar-sized companies? What sort of problems do they hit? This approach is known as reference class forecasting (Flyvbjerg 2006).

How

1. Avoid planning fallacy with reference class forecasting

Flyvbjerg's method requires detailed research so may take some time.

- Find a similar class of projects to yours.
- Find the relevant information for projects in that class – for example, typical budgets and timescale.
- Are there any reasons why your project might be cheaper or quicker than average?
- Decide whether you can justify a more optimistic outlook.

2. Avoid planning fallacy with an outside view

Who can you ask for advice who has attempted a similar project? Ask them to think back to when they were at the same stage you are at now. How do they rate your chances of success? What do they think of your estimates for budget and timescale? How does that compare to your estimate?

3. Carry out a pre-mortem with your team

- Group exercise, 30–40 minutes. You'll need pen and paper, sticky notes, wall space or flip chart.

Give people this scenario:

> 'Imagine we have gone ahead with the project. Twelve months have passed and it has been a total failure. Please write down all the reasons why it failed.'

- Ask everyone to work silently and separately, so they don't influence each other.
- Ask them to write each reason on a separate sticky note.
- After 10 minutes, gather all the sticky notes and arrange them into clusters (you will probably find a number of similar reasons).
- Now as a group determine which reasons are the most important to tackle by arranging them on a matrix – see Section 6.1 for examples.

Turn the most serious problems into 'How could we...?' questions and brainstorm solutions. Keep the list of worst-case scenarios, in case any start to come true.

Reflection

How easy do you find it to be optimistic about your chances of success? What about those around you? What did you notice about the mood of your team during the pre-mortem?

References

Flyvbjerg, B. (2006) From Nobel Prize to project management: Getting risks right, *Project Management Journal,* 37(3), 5–15.
Kahneman, D. (2011) *Thinking, Fast and Slow.* Penguin Books.

Klein, G. (1998) *Sources of Power: How People Make Decisions*. MIT Press.

Thaler, R. and Sunstein, C. (2009) *Nudge: Improving Decisions about Health, Wealth and Happiness*. Penguin Books.

University of Foreign Military and Cultural Studies (2012) *Red Team Handbook*. UFMCS.

6.5 Overconfidence

Why

Confidence is a very attractive trait. We'd all love to be more confident at times. But there's a fine line between confidence based firmly on proven abilities and overconfidence based on delusions. Overconfidence lies at the root of many failures, from getting lost in a part of town we thought we knew to investing billions in dodgy derivatives before a financial crash.

We're not very good at spotting overconfidence, either in our own judgements or in people who we think of as experts. Much human activity is so complex and unpredictable that it defies expert prediction. Looking at how media pundits fail to predict trends in media consumption, TV executive Armando Iannucci observed: 'So much for experts. Their guess is as good as yours, but more expensive.'[13]

---

[13] Armando Iannucci, MacTaggart Lecture at the 2015 Edinburgh International Television Festival: http://tinyurl.com/IannucciSpeech

Knowledge briefing

Philip Tetlock studied political and economic predictions made by expert forecasters over a 20-year period. He found that, once they strayed beyond short-range forecasts, most experts' predictions were little better than random guesses.

Tetlock said experts fall into two camps: hedgehogs and foxes.[14] Hedgehogs know one big thing, they have a theory that explains the world, and are confident of their judgements. Foxes are aware of lots of things, they're sceptical of theories and modest about their conclusions. Foxes made the most reliable forecasters, but Hedgehogs, with their easy-to-explain view of the world, got all the media attention (Tetlock 2005).

However, in a follow-up study, Tetlock found that some people do consistently make accurate predictions about complex situations. These 'superforecasters' have a number of traits: they're open to outside views, they conduct 'unflinching post-mortems' when they get a prediction wrong and they know how to break intractable problems down into smaller questions (Tetlock and Gardner 2015).

Our confidence often stems more from the ease with which we reached our conclusions than the strength of the evidence they were based upon. If information comes easily and vividly to mind, we feel more confident that our case is proved.

Psychologists Daniel Kahneman and Gary Klein identified two factors to consider when deciding whether to trust a confident expert's opinion: does the expert operate in a fairly consistent environment and do they get rapid feedback on their actions? Imagine the difference between steering a jet-ski around a lake and piloting a supertanker into a stormy harbour. You could very quickly trust your 'feel' for one situation but not the other (Kahneman 2011).

---

[14] Tetlock's metaphor comes from philosopher Isaiah Berlin's book, *The Hedgehog and the Fox: An Essay on Tolstoy's View of History*.

Nassim Nicholas Taleb only has time for two kinds of expert: ones who have 'skin in the game' (for example, they put their own money where their mouth is); and those who make judgements based on experimental trial and error rather than abstract theorising (Taleb 2010).

How

1. List 12 reasons why you're confident of your opinion

- Solo exercise, 10–15 minutes. You'll need paper and pen.

Write down 12 reasons why you are confident that you're right. If you find 12 easy, make it 20. Most of us will struggle after five or six.

If we find evidence easily, we are more inclined to feel that something is true. Ironically, the harder you have to search for evidence, the less likely you are to strongly believe it. So this exercise could de-bias your confidence levels and make you more realistic about your project.

2. Are you overconfident?

Questions to ask experts (or yourself) from *Expert Political Judgement* (2006), *The Black Swan* (2010), *Superforecasting* (2015) and *Thinking, Fast and Slow* (2011):

- *Environment:* how consistent is the setting where you learned your expertise? Do the same kind of situations repeat over time? Are there learnable rules?
- *Feedback:* how quickly do you get feedback on your actions? How easily can you adjust your actions in response to feedback?
- *Skin in the game:* what have you got to lose if your expert judgement is wrong?
- *Experimenting or theorising:* how do you test your expertise?
- *Hedgehog:* do you have an overarching theory which explains most facts?

- *Or fox:* do you see the world as a complex place which resists easy explanation?
- *Superforecaster:* do you conduct 'unflinching post-mortems' when your estimates are proved wrong?

Reflection

How do you feel about taking your confidence down a notch?

References

Kahneman, D. (2011) *Thinking, Fast and Slow.* Penguin Books.
Taleb, N.N. (2010) *The Black Swan: The Impact of the Highly Improbable.* Penguin Books.
Tetlock, P. (2005) *Expert Political Judgment: How Good Is It? How Can We Know?* Princeton University Press.
Tetlock, P. and Gardner, D. (2015) *Superforecasting: The Art and Science of Prediction.* Random House.

6.6 The sunk cost fallacy (aka why it's hard to pull the plug)

Why

Have you ever thrown good money after bad? Have you ever kept gambling because you might still win back your early stake? Have you ever kept going down the wrong road, hoping it would turn out to be right, because to turn back now would mean you'd wasted all those miles you've just travelled?

If so, you have first-hand experience of the sunk cost fallacy.

Sunk cost fallacies lie behind many defence contracts, transport schemes and IT programmes which deliver late and over budget. With sunk cost fallacy, our judgement is so skewed by what we stand to lose *right now* that we can't focus on whether it's right to carry on or pull the plug.

Knowledge briefing

Our natural loss aversion is to blame for sunk cost fallacies. Imagine I offer you a gamble on the toss of a coin. If you lose, you will pay me £10,000 of your own money. What would I have to offer you as a prize to make you take that gamble? £10,000? £20,000? £50,000?

Most people want a much higher reward to justify the risk. This is because we feel the pain of potential losses much more acutely than the pleasure of uncertain gains. We also have a substitution bias which tempts us to replace a difficult question – 'what are the chances I can turn this around?' – with an easier one – 'how do I feel about this loss?' (Kahneman 2011).

'No amount of sunk costs can make an erroneous belief accurate,' according to author Kathryn Schulz. But these losses can affect our loyalty towards that belief. The slightest hint of 'I told you so' can reinforce a stubborn determination to cling on to previously held views. 'However much we might enjoy crowing at other people's errors,' writes Schulz, 'it gives people little reason to change their minds and consider sharing our beliefs instead' (Schulz 2015).

It's much more productive to remind everyone that we are all capable of making mistakes. Some organisations consciously reframe their losses as lessons learned, in order to take the sting out of loss aversion (Heffernan 2015).

How

1. Test your own loss aversion

- Group exercise, 10 minutes.

Do this as a very short exercise before any discussion about pulling the plug on a project.

- Offer the group the gamble of losing £10,000 *of their own money* on the toss of a coin.
- Ask everyone to think about it silently for a moment then write down how much they would want as a reward in order to risk taking that bet.
- Go round the group asking for their answers. Explore any differences in reward levels that people would want.

Explain that this is a test for loss aversion, which is common to all of us (therefore there are no 'right' answers to the test). Point out that real, immediate losses are painful, but we can't let this pain cloud our judgement on the right course of action.

Whatever time and money you've spent already on your project is effectively lost, whether you carry on or not. You can't get it back, and there might be even bigger losses if you keep going.

2. Establish some humble ground rules

Explain to the group that any phrase which smacks of 'I told you so' is banned from the discussion, as it will only make people more likely to cling on to previously held views. Remind people that we all make mistakes, nobody's perfect. If you're right this time, you might just have been lucky and it could be your mistake we're discussing next time.

3. Reframe losses as lessons learned

- Solo or group exercise, 40–60 minutes. Worksheet essential.

This technique requires a bit of paper folding in order to physically remove the sight of what you've lost from your discussion of whether to carry on or pull the plug. This also neatly turns the losses into the starting point for a discussion of what lessons you've learned.

- Fill out all the boxes on the first side of the sheet, except the one which asks you to rate your chances of success.

Weed out bad ideas

FOLD ALONG DOTTED LINE

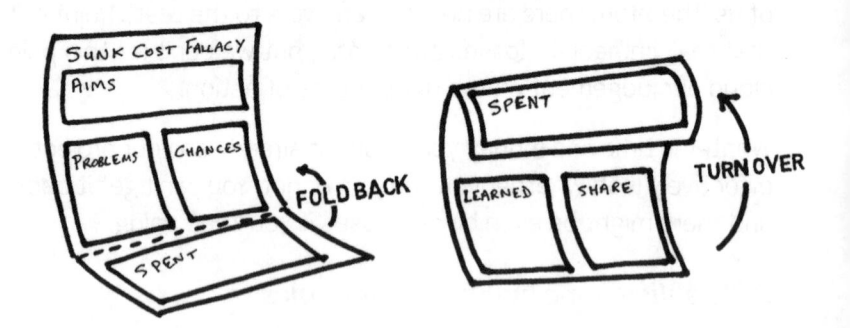

- Fold the worksheet along the dotted line and flip it over. Now the 'spent' box has become the starting point for the questions on the reverse of the sheet.
- Fill out the boxes for what you've learned and who you need to share these lessons with.
- Now you can turn back to the first side of the sheet and discuss the question of whether to carry on or pull the plug.
- Keep the 'spent' box folded out of sight, because your losses up to this point should not determine whether you should carry on or not.

Big picture

SUNK COST FALLACY

ORIGINAL AIMS AND ASSUMPTIONS

PROBLEMS AND POSSIBLE SOLUTIONS

COST OF CONTINUING?

CHANCES OF HITTING ORIGINAL AIMS?

CARRY ON OR PULL THE PLUG?

WHAT WE'VE SPENT SO FAR
TIME
MONEY
RESOURCES

Weed out bad ideas

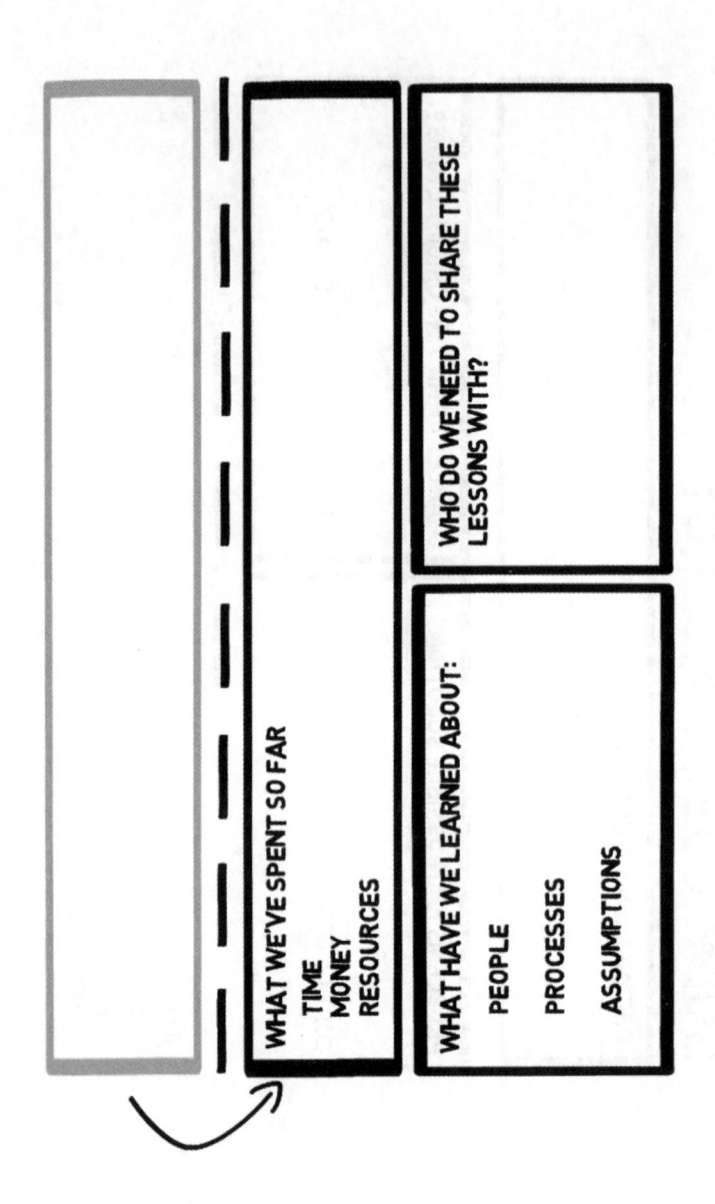

WHAT WE'VE SPENT SO FAR

TIME
MONEY
RESOURCES

WHAT HAVE WE LEARNED ABOUT:

PEOPLE

PROCESSES

ASSUMPTIONS

WHO DO WE NEED TO SHARE THESE LESSONS WITH?

Reflection

How easy is it to remove the pain of what you've definitely lost from your judgement of whether to carry on or pull the plug? Does it help to reframe your losses in terms of what you've learned?

References

Heffernan, M. (2015) *Beyond Measure: The Big Impact of Small Changes*. TED Audio Books.
Kahneman, D. (2011) *Thinking, Fast and Slow*. Penguin Books.
Schulz, K. (2015) *Being Wrong: Adventures in the Margins of Error*. Portobello Publishers.

6.7 How to fail well

Why

Make no mistake, it's very hard to fail well. Despite the fact we all fail at some point in our lives, despite the lessons we could learn, we find our failures incredibly hard to talk about. Mistakes can feel so unpleasant that we'll go to great lengths to avoid making them and deny responsibility for them when we do.

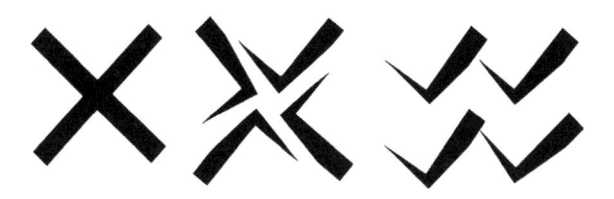

But there's a more optimistic view of mistakes: as lessons to be learned, as staging posts towards something better, and as part of what it means to grow as a human being. You may be able to get some benefit when things inevitably go wrong somewhere along the line. But you should be aware that failure will always be tricky emotional territory for you and others.

A 'well-intentioned failure' should be seen as a source of learning, not shame, according to business writer Margaret Heffernan. This is an important qualification – we're talking here about people who made mistakes but meant well at the time. If they were being deliberately reckless or malicious (and this does happen), that's a different case. In fact, it's a disciplinary matter and falls outside this book's remit.

Knowledge briefing

Organisations that promote 'just cultures' discuss failures with the same humble and generous mindset as they discuss new ideas. Some companies make a point of recording all mistakes and sharing them with other staff. This sends out two messages: nobody's perfect, and when we admit a mistake we're on the path to putting it right (Heffernan 2015).

Many successful and highly educated people have never learned how to learn from failure, according to Chris Argyris. Rather than reflecting on how their thinking may be at fault, they become defensive and blame anyone but themselves when things go badly. 'Their ability to learn shuts down precisely at the moment they need it most,' he writes. Leaders need to set an example that it's okay to reflect on the thoughts and emotions behind decisions. We need to see this questioning of our thinking as 'not a sign of mistrust or an invasion of privacy but as a valuable opportunity for learning' (Argyris 1991).

We can improve our ability to bounce back from failures. Resilience, according to Carol Dweck, comes from having a growth mindset rather than a fixed mindset. Someone with a fixed mindset tends to see abilities as innate, they're used to being told they are good (or not good) at a certain task. They react to failure by doubting themselves.

A growth mindset means you think ability comes from practice. You can encourage a growth mindset by praising process rather than personality ('you've worked hard at this' rather than 'you're good at this'). People with a growth mindset react to failure by doubting the process, and therefore are more willing to try again in a different way (Dweck 2006).

You can achieve more in failing to hit an ambitious target than succeeding at a more modest goal, according to Laszlo Bock, head of HR at Google. This is one of the justifications behind

Big picture

Google's 'moon-shots' such as driverless cars and Google Glass. Bock's 'Rules for Screwing Up' include: 'Admit your mistake. Be transparent . . . Fix whatever broke. Find the moral in the mistake and teach it' (Bock 2015).

Most authors agree you should have a good post-mortem when a project has finished or failed. Try to include outside observers, as they are better placed to see where you have jumped to conclusions based on scant evidence.

You should do post-mortems for your successes too. Who knows, your success might just have been down to luck (Kahneman 2011).

How

1. Hold a good post-mortem

- Group exercise, 30–40 minutes.

For this exercise:

- Set the right tone for discussing mistakes (see Section 6.6).
- Invite outside observers to join in if possible.
- Remember that good post-mortems lead to action.
- Try one of these worksheets:

Alternatively, you could use the sunk cost fallacy worksheet (Section 6.6) for your post-mortem. Replace 'Should we carry on or pull the plug?' with 'How could we do this better next time?'

THREE DIFFERENT WAYS TO HOLD A POST-MORTEM

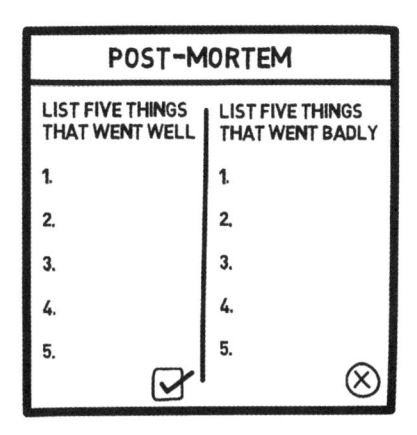

POST-MORTEM	
LIST FIVE THINGS THAT WENT WELL	LIST FIVE THINGS THAT WENT BADLY
1.	1.
2.	2.
3.	3.
4.	4.
5.	5.

Weed out bad ideas

LOVE, LEARN AND LEAVE BEHIND

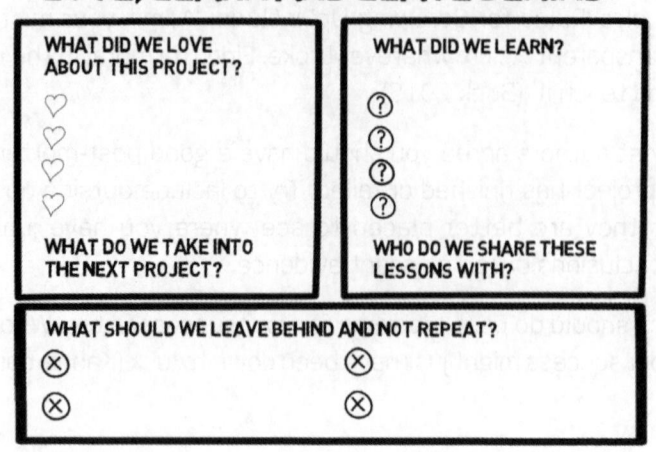

| WHAT DID WE LOVE ABOUT THIS PROJECT? ♡ ♡ ♡ ♡ WHAT DO WE TAKE INTO THE NEXT PROJECT? | WHAT DID WE LEARN? ⑦ ⑦ ⑦ ⑦ WHO DO WE SHARE THESE LESSONS WITH? |

| WHAT SHOULD WE LEAVE BEHIND AND NOT REPEAT? ⊗ ⊗ ⊗ ⊗ |

'FIND THE MORAL IN THE MISTAKE AND TEACH IT'
LASZLO BOCK, GOOGLE

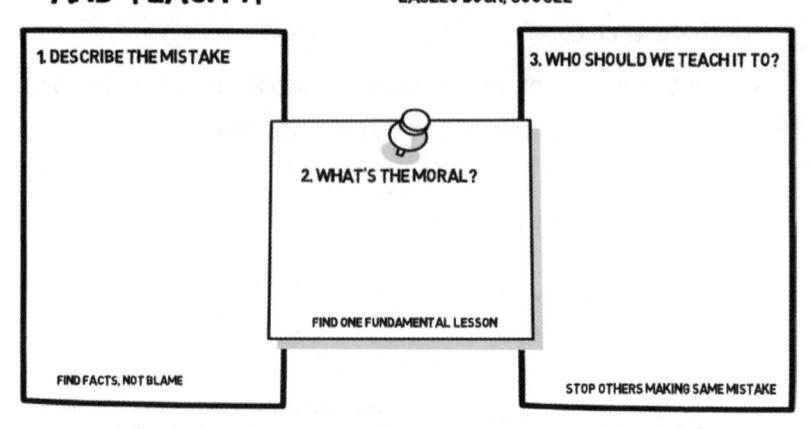

| 1. DESCRIBE THE MISTAKE | 3. WHO SHOULD WE TEACH IT TO? |

2. WHAT'S THE MORAL?

FIND ONE FUNDAMENTAL LESSON

FIND FACTS, NOT BLAME

STOP OTHERS MAKING SAME MISTAKE

2. Promote a growth mindset

Follow these tips from Carol Dweck:

- *Praise wisely:* reward good efforts, strategies and progress rather than praising people for being bright or right.
- *Reframe difficult* as getting out of your comfort zone and building new skills.
- Use *'not right yet'* instead of 'failed', so there's still a chance to improve.

Reflection

What kind of post-mortems have you carried out in the past? What do you gain from them? How do you feel about discussing your own well-intentioned failures?

References

Argyris, C. (1991) Teaching smart people how to learn, *Harvard Business Review,* May–June.

Bock, L. (2015) *Work Rules! Insights from Google that Will Transform How You Live and Lead.* John Murray.

Dweck, C.S. (2006) *Mindset: The New Psychology of Success.* Ballantine Books.

Heffernan, M. (2015) *Beyond Measure: The Big Impact of Small Changes.* TED Audio Books.

Kahneman, D. (2011) *Thinking, Fast and Slow.* Penguin Books.

Chapter 7

Sell your best ideas

- **7.1** You, your audience, your message
- **7.2** Real, original, simple
- **7.3** Three is the magic number (and other rhetorical devices)
- **7.4** Go viral
- **7.5** Great stories
- **7.6** Road-test your story
- **7.7** Hand over the spark

SPEED READ
7. Sell your best ideas

7.1 You, your audience, your message

Whether you stand up and make presentations, write reports or seek attention on social media, you have to learn how to sell your best ideas to the people who matter.

It's no use having a brilliant idea if you can't get anyone to listen to it. But before you get into the detail of your message you need to think about yourself and your audience. Why are *you* trying to get our attention? What is driving *you* to reach out to us?

Ultimately, you want your audience to love your story so much that they go away and tell it to others. Get your audience on your side, then it's much easier to explain the detail and logic behind your idea.

When you get on to the details of your message, think about how you write and speak. Do you sound natural or do you use jargon and business buzzwords?

Sell your best ideas

> **Do this**
> Listen to yourself and the people around you. Who speaks or writes clearly? What impact do they have on others?

7.2 Real, original, simple

We see or hear up to 100,000 words each day. You're not the only one trying to tell a story. How are you going to make yours heard above the din?

How often do you find yourself falling back on cliches? They often contain a kernel of truth. But they can also make people switch off. People stop listening because they assume they know what you're going to say next. If you want to say something new and distinctive, cliches work against you.

It's harder to use cliches if you keep your message real. Use images, physical objects and everyday language as much as you can, rather than abstract terms. Look closely at what's going on and describe it in your own words. Don't reach for ready-made terms that others have coined: you'll find their value has already been spent.

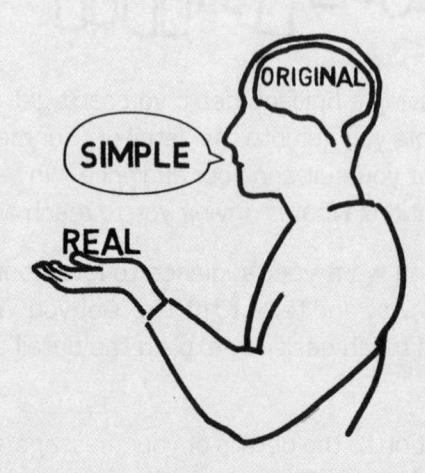

Keep it simple. The ultimate respect you can pay your audience is to show you value their time. Use as little of it as possible. Leave them wanting more.

> **Do this**
> Think about how you describe your work. When do you use cliches, jargon or abstract terms? What do you think when you hear other people talk like this?

7.3 Three is the magic number (and other rhetorical devices)

People have been studying how to craft a strong message since ancient Greek times. The lessons of rhetoric still hold true today. Use them to hone your message and not only will people listen, but more importantly, they'll remember the points you want them to.

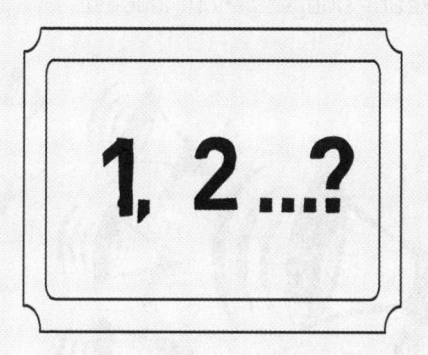

1, 2 ...?

In this section, we look at three commonly used rhetorical devices you can use to get your ideas across: *repetition*, *omission* and *reframing*. Why just three? Because it seems three is the magic number. Repetition in threes establishes a pattern without becoming a list. It provides rhythm and a structure which helps your audience anticipate what's coming next.

Sometimes the most powerful part of the message is the one that is left unsaid. Omission invites the audience to fill in the gap. We're more likely to remember a message if we've had to do some work on it ourselves. Sometimes it's the frame around the message we remember most, especially when powerful reframing makes us see the world differently.

> **Do this**
> Think about the messages you remember most strongly from other projects. What elements stuck in your mind? What phrases or rhetorical devices made them stick?

7.4 Go viral

In theory, the internet levels the communications playing field and allows anyone with zero budget to reach an audience of millions. But there are so many messages out there on so many platforms that an older business model has reasserted itself: those with the biggest marketing budgets shout loudest.

There's a lot you can learn from studying the kinds of messages that do go viral. You need to understand why people share online. What are we trying to say about ourselves when we share with others? How can we get other people to share our message? What results or reaction do we want to achieve?

> **Do this**
> Write down a list of all the things you've shared online in the last couple of days. What made you share them? Who did you share them with?

7.5 Great stories

The simplest and quickest way to get people to listen to your idea is to tell it like a story. This doesn't mean turning every report and spreadsheet into a fire-side tale. But it does mean learning from the power of great stories to hook audiences.

Great storytellers recycle great stories. Some are direct adaptations, like setting *Hamlet* in a biker gang (*Sons of Anarchy*). Others echo down the ages because they reflect universal human needs. You can exploit a handful of techniques from great stories and use them to hone your message.

You can focus on the hero of a story and how he or she changes. You can cast people around you in the roles of mentors, allies and enemies. You can describe your project as a journey towards a final goal. You can think of triggers, setbacks, choices and climaxes. Not only will this help you express your ideas, it could actually help you make them stronger.

> **Do this**
>
> How often do people where you work use great stories to hold an audience? How do you feel when someone takes this approach with you? What's the last great story you just had to retell to others?

7.6 Road-test your story

The best way to test if your story is working is to tell it. Start with friends or colleagues. Then move on to people who probably couldn't care less. If you can hold their attention – better still, get them leaning in and asking questions – you are doing well.

Is your story relatable to real life and everyday experience? Is it immersive? Is it memorable? Does it appeal to emotion as well as reason?

There are simple tests you can do on the actual language you use. Put samples of your writing through online readability tests like the Gunning Fog Index or SMOG (Simple Measure of Gobbledegook).

The higher your score, the less accessible your writing is to the widest audience. A high score means you're asking people to put in a lot more effort to understand you. Advanced and technical writing might be essential, given the nature of your project. But it might just be bad writing.

> **Do this**
> Take the last lengthy email or report you wrote about your project and put the text through word cloud software. How prominent is jargon or business-speak?

7.7 Hand over the spark

One final trick from the storytellers: learn how to hand over the spark that ignited your passion in the first place. If you are in the early stages of a project or creative process, you could be in for a long haul. You need to convince your backers and buyers that you are committed to seeing it through, and that means showing them why you care.

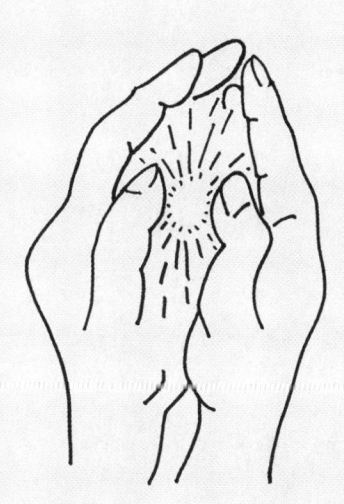

This might mean giving something away about yourself, allowing something personal to creep into the story. It might mean showing how your idea has brought about a change in you.

Sell your best ideas

If you get this right, you won't just get people to back your project. You will hand the spark over to them and ignite their passion for your project too.

> **Do this**
> Ask yourself why you really care about your project. What was the spark that ignited your passion?

BIG PICTURE
7. Sell your best ideas

7.1 You, your audience, your message

Why

If you want to get people to back your idea, first you've got to get them to listen. When we're on the receiving end of someone else's idea, often in the back of our minds we're thinking: 'Hang on a second. Who is this and why should I care?' So the first thing you have to establish is who you are and why you deserve a hearing.

The next thing to work out is what your audience needs from you. Show that you've paid attention to their expectations and their values.

Speak in terms that they will understand. Ditch the dull language of corporate communications and talk like a human being. Even if your audience uses corporate-speak, you'll be doing them a favour, and giving them a refreshing change, by using everyday language instead.

Knowledge briefing

Long before spin doctors, TED talks or press releases were invented, the ancient Greeks had worked out the art of getting your message across. Aristotle's rhetoric identified three key elements of a persuasive argument:

- *Ethos:* appeal to your character and values. Why are *you* speaking to us?
- *Pathos:* appeal to your audience's feelings. Why should *we* listen to you?
- *Logos:* the logic and reasons behind your argument.

If you neglect ethos and pathos, you've lost your audience, no matter how strong the logos of your argument (Aristotle, 4th century BC).

'People who write well, do well,' according to copywriters Kenneth Roman and Joel Raphaelson. Often the first and only impression we make is through our words. Woolly writing and woolly speech show woolly thinking. If you're at the top of your field, you must make yourself clear to those who aren't. If you're on your way up, you must show others they can trust you. Either way, you must write clearly and with purpose (Roman and Raphaelson 2000).

How

1. Work out why you write so badly

Bad writing may actually be caused by fear. Many of us have 'imposter syndrome', a fear that we don't really belong and will soon be found out. We try to fit in by copying the jargon and phrases we hear around us. Then there's the fear that what we need to say will hurt the listener. So we reach for euphemisms like 'downsizing'. The pain is still there, but with added mistrust.

Big picture

When you sit down to write or stand up to speak, what are you afraid of? Make a note of these fears before you start. They are like red flags, predicting bad writing.

2. Think about ethos and pathos as well as logos

- Group or solo exercise, 20–30 minutes. Worksheet optional.

Create two large boxes, labelled 'ethos' and 'pathos'.

- In the 'ethos' box write down what you believe in. What are your values? Why does this make you act the way you do? (If you're not sure about the values behind your project, try the tools in Chapter 2.)
- In the 'pathos' box, what about your audience? What are their values? What language do they feel comfortable with? How can you appeal to their emotions?
- Finally, write a single line for your main argument – your 'logos'.

Highlight anything in the 'ethos' and 'pathos' boxes that helps you introduce or reinforce your argument.

ETHOS, PATHOS AND LOGOS

ETHOS: YOUR CHARACTER AND VALUES
WHY ARE YOU SPEAKING TO US?

PATHOS: YOUR AUDIENCE'S THOUGHTS AND FEELINGS
WHY SHOULD WE LISTEN?

LOGOS: THE REASONS BEHIND YOUR ARGUMENT
HOW MIGHT YOU CONVINCE US?

3. Borrow from 20th-century masters of prose

> 'Short words are best and the old words, when short, best of all.'
>
> (Winston Churchill)

Look at the long words you are using. Can you replace them and still make sense? Now what about the modern jargon – do you really need it? Will the audience understand it?

> 'Never use the passive when you can use the active.'
>
> (George Orwell)

Passive means fudge, allowing responsibility to be evaded. Don't write 'concerns were escalated', tell us who said what to whom. Go through your writing. Find any instance where it isn't clear who's responsible for specific actions. Why are you fudging the issue? What are you trying to protect? If you are writing in a passive voice, delete it and use the active voice instead.

> 'Write the way you talk. Naturally. Never use jargon words like reconceptualize, attitudinally, judgementally. They are hallmarks of a pretentious ass.'
>
> (David Ogilvy)

Enough said. Find the jargon and strike it out.

Reflection

How does focusing on your audience alter the way you structure your message? What's important to them – and how does that differ from what's important to you?

References

Aristotle (1991) *Rhetoric* (trans W. Rhys Roberts). Penguin Classics.
Roman, K. and Raphaelson, J. (2000) *Writing that Works: How to Communicate Effectively in Business.* HarperCollins.

7.2 Real, original, simple

Why

How many times have you glazed over while listening to a speaker or mentally wandered off while reading a paragraph? Maybe you struggle through, but you start to resent the person who's making you do it. If you want people to listen – and better still, to remember – then you need to make your message real, original and simple.

Knowledge briefing

Corporate cultures often value written reports and spoken presentations over sensory experiences. But showing a prototype of your idea, no matter how crude, appeals to different learning styles and encourages others to build on an idea they can see right in front of them (Allan et al. 2002).

George Orwell argued that resorting to cliches and well-worn phrases means letting someone else's words do your thinking for you. Orwell advised writers to 'put off using words as long as possible and get one's meaning as clear as one can through pictures and sensations'. Only then should you reach for the words that best describe the image in your head, rather than use an existing figure of speech. This is how Orwell visualised a cliche-bound writer: 'an accumulation of stale phrases chokes him like tea leaves blocking a sink' (Orwell 1946).

Good copywriters know that less is more. Simplification is part of their craft. It means 'finding the one simple thing to say and illustrating it with total clarity', according to Dominic Gettins. You have to be ruthless with your own message, because no-one else will correct you if it's too wordy. They'll just stop listening (Gettins 2000).

How

1. Make it real

- Group or solo exercise, 30–40 minutes.

How can you bring your idea to life?

- *Prototype:* what can you make, however crude, that shows your project in action?
- *Substitute:* what can you use as a physical 'stand-in' to represent an intangible idea? For example, if you want new training programmes at work, give your audience unfamiliar DIY tools and ask, 'When I give you a new tool for doing your job, what does it feel like? How long would it take to become adept at using it?' You are introducing the metaphor of training-as-tool, and reinforcing it with physical sensation.
- *Role play:* how can you act out a conversation or scenario about your project?
- *Road-test:* how can you road-test your idea and show the results? Can you use video or photographs to show how real people react to your idea?

2. Make it original

- Group or solo exercise, 30–40 minutes. You'll need pen and paper; worksheet optional.

Using George Orwell's four simple questions.

Big picture

- What am I trying to say?
- What words will express it?
- What image or idiom will make it clearer?
- Is this image fresh enough to have an effect?

Try this worksheet as a way of coming up with lots of different images and idioms, then see which ones help you craft a fresh image for your message.

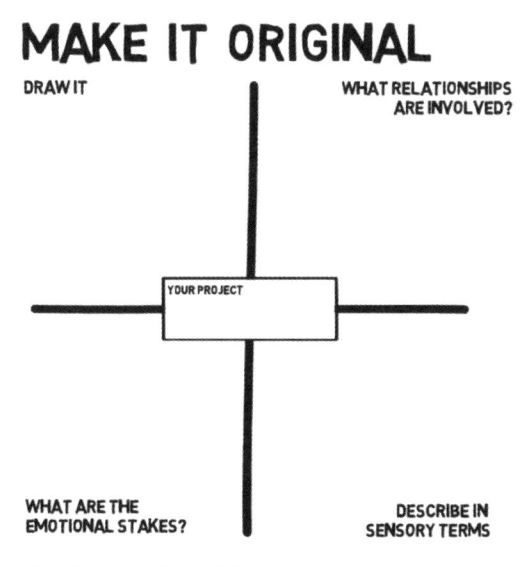

MAKE IT ORIGINAL

- DRAW IT
- WHAT RELATIONSHIPS ARE INVOLVED?
- YOUR PROJECT
- WHAT ARE THE EMOTIONAL STAKES?
- DESCRIBE IN SENSORY TERMS

'GET ONE'S MEANING AS CLEAR AS ONE CAN THROUGH PICTURES AND SENSATIONS' – GEORGE ORWELL

3. Make it simple

- Group or solo exercise, 30–40 minutes. You'll need pen and paper.

Using guidelines from good copywriters (Gettins 2000; Lynch 2014), go through your first draft with a red pen looking for the following:

- *Passive language:* replace it with active.
- *Parentheses (sentences within sentences):* break these into shorter sentences.

Sell your best ideas

- *Cliches:* 'Kill as many cliches as you can. They are not an endangered species.'
- *Long words:* try a short one instead. Strike anything with more than three syllables unless it's absolutely essential.
- *Dead verbs:* why 'deliver improvement' when you can just 'improve'?
- *Abstract nouns:* make your abstract relate to real people, things and places.
- *Nouns as verbs:* waterfalls cascade, humans don't – nor do we action, impact or task.

We will leave the last word to George Orwell:

> 'If it is possible to cut a word out, always cut it out ... any words that don't contribute meaning to a passage dilute its power. Less is always better. Always.'

Reflection

How does the first draft of your message compare to the real, original and simple version?

References

Allan, D., Kingdon, M., Murrin, K. and Rudkin, D. (2002) *Sticky Wisdom: How to Start a Creative Revolution at Work.* ?WhatIf! Publications.

Gettins, D. (2000) *How to Write Great Copy: Learn the Unwritten Rules of Copywriting.* Kogan Page.

Lynch, C. (2014) Business writers, here's why you really need to master the parts of speech: http://www.dorisandbertie.com/goodcopybadcopy/2011/06/14/business-writers-heres-why-you-really-need-to-master-the-parts-of-speech/

Orwell, G. (1946) *Politics and the English Language.* Horizon.

7.3 Three is the magic number (and other rhetorical devices)

Why

Think of any memorable speech or piece of writing. The person behind it almost certainly used rhetorical devices to get their message to stick. These devices don't write your message for you, but they can improve its style and make it memorable.

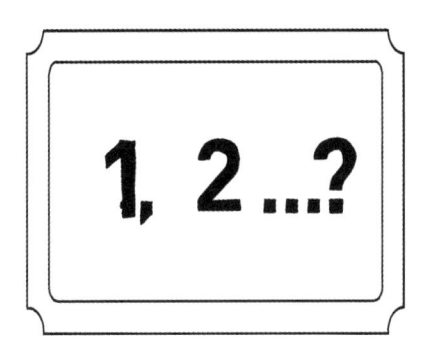

In this section we'll look at three devices: patterns of three, omission and reframing. You can use each one to make your message stand out.

Knowledge briefing

We use short-term working memory to process words as we listen, but we only retain about a quarter of what we hear. Our brains use pattern recognition to work out which bits to keep hold of (Treasure 2011). Grouping words in threes – a tricolon – is used extensively, for example: 'A Mars a day helps you work, rest and play'; 'Veni, vidi, vici'; 'Life, liberty and the pursuit of happiness'. This is because dividing complex subjects into three helps us remember details (Gallo 2014).

Leaving gaps can sometimes make a message stronger. Omission works because we subconsciously want the world to make sense, and so we rush to fill any gaps in a story (Kahneman 2011).

Ernest Hemingway demonstrated this perfectly with his heartbreaking six-word story:

'For sale. Baby shoes. Never worn.'

Reframing or redefining the terms of a situation requires mental effort, which we usually tend to avoid (Kahneman 2011). But reframing is so powerful it can affect the way we think or act. The UK government's Behavioural Insights Team (aka the Nudge Unit) added 100,000 organ donors a year to the transplant register just by asking potential donors if they would accept a donor organ if they needed one themselves. They reframed the situation to make people think of themselves as potential recipients as well as donors (Behavioural Insights Team 2014).

How

1. Organise your thinking in threes

- Group or solo exercise, 30-40 minutes.

Write a short summary of your project. Make sure it's clear and jargon free (try the Tweet simplicity exercise in Section 2.7). Now write three sub-headings: 'Reasons why', 'Tricky issues' and 'Next steps'. Beneath each heading, write three more statements or questions. Rewrite them and keep rewriting until they are all short and simple. Now look back over everything you've written. Chances are your audience will only remember three things you tell them so what should those three things be?

THINKING IN THREES

SUMMARY		
REASONS WHY 1. 2. 3.	**TRICKY ISSUES** 1. 2. 3.	**NEXT STEPS** 1. 2. 3.

Big picture

2. Omission – leave them wanting more

- Group or solo exercise, 30–40 minutes. You'll need pen and paper.

Write a first draft of your idea. Now go through and ask:

- What could I leave out?
- How could I hint at what's been left out?
- What gaps would people try to fill for themselves?
- How can I make them ask 'What happens next?' or 'How did we get here?'
- How would I leave them wanting more?

Or can you copy Hemingway? Write your message in just six words.

3. Reframing – change what you see and say about your project

- Group or solo exercise, 30–40 minutes. You'll need paper and pen, thesaurus; worksheet optional.

Write a description of your project in the centre of the page. Draw a frame around this. Outside the frame, write as many different ways as you can of seeing your project. Think how other people might see it. On the other side, write all the different words you could use to describe it.

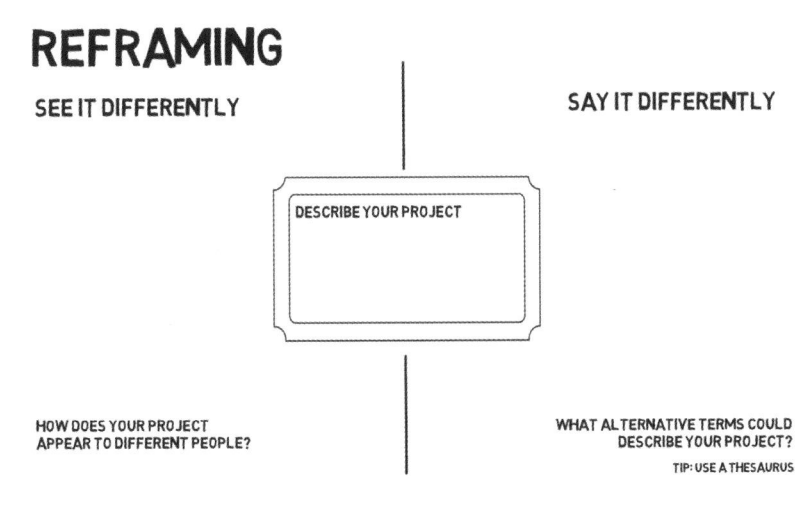

REFRAMING

SEE IT DIFFERENTLY | **SAY IT DIFFERENTLY**

DESCRIBE YOUR PROJECT

HOW DOES YOUR PROJECT APPEAR TO DIFFERENT PEOPLE? | WHAT ALTERNATIVE TERMS COULD DESCRIBE YOUR PROJECT?
TIP: USE A THESAURUS

Now see if any of these alternatives give you a way to reframe your project.

> **Tip**
>
> Use a thesaurus to find antonyms (words which mean the opposite).

Reflection

Compare your message with your first draft. Has it improved? Try it out on friends and supportive colleagues. What do they find memorable?

References

Behavioural Insights Team (2014) *EAST: Four Simple Ways to Apply Behavioural Insights.* Cabinet Office.
Gallo, C. (2014) *Talk Like TED: The 9 Public Speaking Secrets of the World's Top Minds.* Macmillan.
Kahneman, D. (2011) *Thinking, Fast and Slow.* Penguin Books.
Treasure, J. (2011) Five ways to listen better. TED Talks.

7.4 Go viral

Why

Good communication is about getting the right information to the right person at the right time. But on the internet, information can take on a life of its own as soon as people start sharing with others.

We share because we like the buzz we get when people listen to us. What we share depends on the content of the message *and* what we're trying to say about ourselves.

Knowledge briefing

Talking and sharing are fundamental human behaviours, according to Jonah Berger. We are most likely to share positive messages which arouse strong emotions. Berger identified six ingredients likely to make a message spread widely online: 'ideas that contain *Social Currency* and are *Triggered, Emotional, Public, Practically Valuable* and are wrapped into *Stories*' (Berger 2013).

We often share to prove something about ourselves: how smart we are, how caring, how funny or that we are part of a gang. Sharing can be 'emotional gifting', according to Michael Stevens, founder of Vsauce (14 million subscribers on YouTube). We try to improve our relationships with other people by offering them useful information (Stevens 2015).

A *New York Times* study found six different types of sharing persona, each with their own motivations for sharing. Those included wanting to be seen as helpful, intelligent, part of a conversation and creative (New York Times Customer Insight Group 2015).

How

1. Think about why people share messages online

- Group or solo exercise, 30–40 minutes.

Think how sharing messages about your project could help people show themselves in a good light. Can your message be an 'emotional gift' to someone else? Can your message give other people practically valuable advice, such as how to save time or money? How will you make people connect with each other, not just with you?

If the message includes content which is:	I share it because I want the recipient to feel:	Sharing helps me look:
Unexpected	Shocked, surprised	Like the first to know, an insider
Funny	Amused, cheered up	Humorous
Awe-inspiring	Inspired, uplifted	Well informed, clever
Compassionate	Caring, moved	Like I share the same values as you
Angry	Outraged	Provocative, motivated
Practically valuable	Grateful	Pragmatic, considerate

2. Increase the chances your message will spread

- Group or solo exercise, 30–40 minutes. You'll need copies of the worksheet.

This tool will direct you to other chapters in the book that you can use to make your viral message more shareable.

VIRAL MESSAGE DECISION TOOL

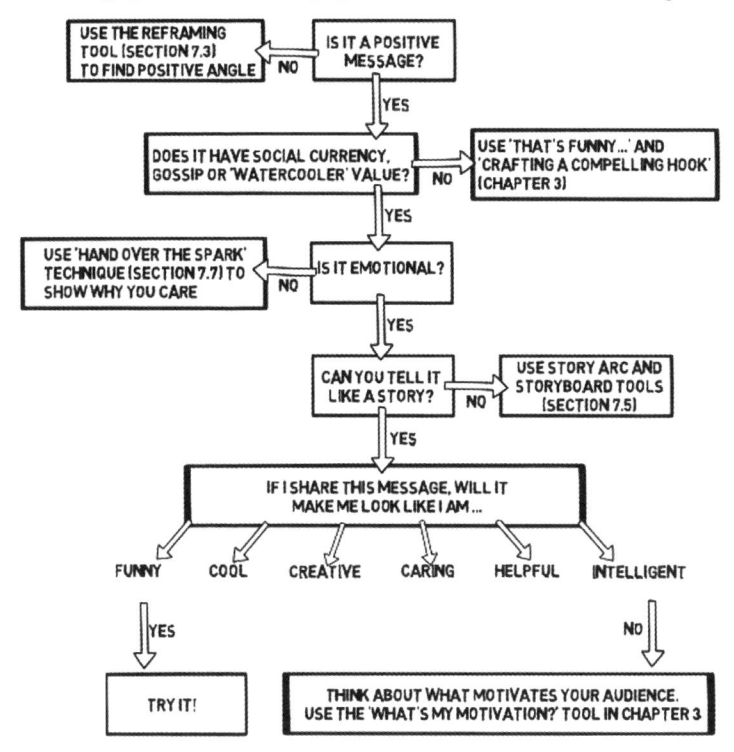

```
IS IT A POSITIVE MESSAGE?
  NO → USE THE REFRAMING TOOL (SECTION 7.3) TO FIND POSITIVE ANGLE
  YES ↓
DOES IT HAVE SOCIAL CURRENCY, GOSSIP OR 'WATERCOOLER' VALUE?
  NO → USE 'THAT'S FUNNY...' AND 'CRAFTING A COMPELLING HOOK' (CHAPTER 3)
  YES ↓
IS IT EMOTIONAL?
  NO → USE 'HAND OVER THE SPARK' TECHNIQUE (SECTION 7.7) TO SHOW WHY YOU CARE
  YES ↓
CAN YOU TELL IT LIKE A STORY?
  NO → USE STORY ARC AND STORYBOARD TOOLS (SECTION 7.5)
  YES ↓
IF I SHARE THIS MESSAGE, WILL IT MAKE ME LOOK LIKE I AM...
  FUNNY / COOL / CREATIVE / CARING / HELPFUL / INTELLIGENT
  YES → TRY IT!
  NO → THINK ABOUT WHAT MOTIVATES YOUR AUDIENCE. USE THE 'WHAT'S MY MOTIVATION?' TOOL IN CHAPTER 3
```

Reflection

Try out the viral version of your message as a blog heading or social media post. Does it get a greater response than normal?

References

Berger, J. (2013) *Contagious: Why Things Catch On.* Simon & Schuster.
New York Times Customer Insight Group (2015) *The Psychology of Sharing.* New York Times.
Stevens, M. (2015) Speech to Children's Media Conference, UK, July.

7.5 Great stories

Why

We are utterly hooked on stories from early childhood. We feel our favourite hero's triumphs, we mourn their losses. We think of our favourite soap opera characters as real-life neighbours. Advertisers, politicians and campaigners have become expert storytellers to capitalise on this.

Use some of the storyteller's magic to make people see your project in a new light. Keep them hooked right up to the (happy) end.

Knowledge briefing

Our minds evolved to make sense of the world and predict what's going to happen next. The simplest way of doing this is to arrange information in a story.

We all understand the rhythm of beginning, middle and end; we can all imagine seeing the world through a story character's eyes (Cron 2012).

Facts alone activate the language-processing parts of our brain. Stories activate sensory, visual and motor areas too. It's like we are living the story in our heads as we hear it (Gallo 2014).

Only a few types of story are repeated across cultures, according to Christopher Booker. Their common features include a hero who is called on a journey; enemies, allies and mentors; a climax and a final resolution – the happy or unhappy ending (Booker 2009). If you want to turn your project into an engaging story, you should cast your audience or customer as the hero while you take on the role of mentor (Sachs 2012).

Storytellers who use a 'cold open' grab attention straight away. This means they cut to the action first, before explaining how we got to that point (think of any Bond movie or the first five minutes of *Breaking Bad*). 'Give us the best you've got in the first few minutes,' says ad-man John Weich. 'We'll decide then and there if you're worthy of our precious attention' (Weich 2013).

You can structure factual information in the same way as a story without compromising its accuracy. The BBC's Natural History Unit uses story techniques to make their wildlife programmes more emotionally engaging for viewers. Storytelling helps, according to story consultant Hazel Marshall, 'otherwise we've just got information, which may be fascinating, but the only people who are going to be into that are people who already love that area' (Marshall 2015).

How

1. What are the core elements of your story?

- Group or solo exercise, 30–40 minutes.

Answer these questions, imagining that your project is a story:

- Who is the hero of your story? (Spoiler: it's not you.)
- What kind of guide or mentor are you?
- How is your project going to help the hero?
- What obstacles must the hero overcome?
- How does your hero change by the end of your story?
- What's the moral of your story?
- How do you want people to feel at the end?

Sell your best ideas

2. Turn your idea into a story arc

- Group or solo exercise, 30–40 minutes. You'll need paper and pen, and copies of the worksheet.

Who is the hero of your story? Plot their journey through a typical story arc. Remember to show how your hero should change by the end of the arc.

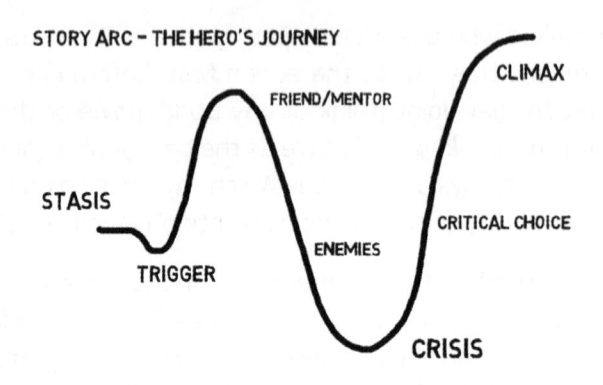

STORY ARC – THE HERO'S JOURNEY

- STASIS
- TRIGGER
- FRIEND/MENTOR
- ENEMIES
- CRISIS
- CRITICAL CHOICE
- CLIMAX

STASIS: WHERE YOUR HERO STARTS

TRIGGER: WHAT MAKES HERO DECIDE TO CHANGE?

FRIEND/MENTOR: WHO HELPS THEM ON THEIR JOURNEY?

ENEMIES: WHO OPPOSES THEM?

CRISIS: WHAT ARE THE SETBACKS?

CRITICAL CHOICE: WHAT MUST YOUR HERO DECIDE?

CLIMAX: HOW DOES THE JOURNEY RESOLVE? HOW HAS YOUR HERO CHANGED?

3. Turn your story on its head

- Group or solo exercise, 30–40 minutes. You'll need paper and pen, and large sticky notes.

Take each moment on your story arc and write it on a separate sticky note. Now rearrange the order. What would people think if you started at the end? Or in the middle of the action? Would a 'cold open' grab their attention long enough to explain how we got to that point?

4. Turn your idea into a Pixar six-step storyboard

- Group or solo exercise, 30–40 minutes. You'll need paper and pen, and copies of the worksheet.

Decide who your hero is and put them through the six stages used by Pixar storyboard artist Emma Coats. How does your role as mentor help the hero? How does he or she change?

PIXAR STORYBOARD

1. ONCE UPON A TIME …	2. EVERY DAY…	3. ONE DAY…
4. BECAUSE OF THAT…	5. BECAUSE OF THAT…	6. UNTIL FINALLY…

Source: Based on Coats (2012).

Reflection

How does it feel casting yourself as mentor in a story? How could this alter the way you approach your 'hero', for example, your clients or stakeholders? How are you promising to help them change?

References

Booker, C. (2009) *The Seven Basic Plots: Why We Tell Stories.* Continuum.

Coats, E. (2012) 22 #storybasics I've picked up in my time at Pixar: http://tinyurl.com/EmmaCoatsPixarRules

Cron, L. (2012) *Wired for Story: The Writer's Guide to Using Brain Science to Hook Readers from the Very First Sentence.* Ten Speed Press.

Gallo, C. (2014) *Talk Like TED: The 9 Public Speaking Secrets of the World's Top Minds.* Macmillan.

Marshall, H. (2015) Natural narratives. BBC Academy website: http://tinyurl.com/bbcstorytelling

Sachs, J. (2012) *Winning the Story Wars: Why Those Who Tell – and Live – the Best Stories Will Rule the Future.* Harvard Business School Publishing.

Weich, J. (2013) *Storytelling on Steroids: 10 Stories that Hijacked the Pop Culture Conversation.* BIS Publishers.

7.6 Road-test your story

Why

Nobody's ideas are perfect at first, nor is anybody's story. The sooner you can test your story, the sooner you can start improving it. All the effort you've put into your new idea will be wasted if you can't hold people's attention long enough to tell them about it.

Most of us are genuinely interested in what other people do. It makes for good conversation and, after all, there may be something in it for us. That gives you lots of opportunities to try your story out and see what response you get.

Work out what you're going to say when someone asks, 'So what are you up to these days then?'

Knowledge briefing

Networking expert David Thomas advises that very early in the story you tell about yourself or your work, you should offer something that might satisfy your listener's needs. You're inviting them to realise they want what you've got. This makes them come to you with questions and that makes your job much easier (Thomas 2015).

Hollywood writer Blake Snyder would pitch new script ideas to strangers in a coffee queue, saying, 'Hi, can you help me, I'm working on a movie idea and I wanted to know what you think.' He'd watch their reaction to his extreme version of the elevator pitch. If their eyes started to wander, he knew his plot still needed fixing (Snyder 2005).

Marketer Jonah Sachs argues that irresistible stories should pass the tests of being tangible, relatable, immersive, memorable and emotional. His final test is: 'Does your communication make you feel something rather than just think something?' (Sachs 2012).

The Simple Measure of Gobbledygook (SMOG) scores your writing for complexity, based on sentence structure and word length. The Gunning Fog Index shows the average reading age your audience will need to understand your message. Both tests are freely available online and will rank your text on a scale from simple road sign up to Shakespearean prose (http://www.thewriter.com/what-we-think/readability-checker/).

How

1. Prepare your own elevator pitch

- Solo exercise, 30 minutes. You'll need paper and pen, and a stopwatch.

You've got 30 seconds, that's roughly 90 words. What are you going to say that will hook attention and neatly summarise what you're working on? How can you appeal to what your audience needs? What will make them come back at you with a question? For example, I can say, 'I run a training business that helps people who are stuck for new ideas.' Hopefully, most people will think: 'Oh, I sometimes get stuck for new ideas, I wonder how you could help me?'

Get your stopwatch ready. Stand in front of a mirror and go: 'Hi, what are you up to these days? [pause] Me? Well, I'm . . .' [start timer].

2. Put your text through an online test

Paste your text into the online readability checker at http://www.thewriter.com/what-we-think/readability-checker/. This entire chapter has a Gunning Fog score of 7.8 which means the average 13-year-old should be able to understand it.

3. Put your story through Jonah Sachs' TRIME test

- Group or solo exercise, 30–40 minutes. You'll need pen and paper, and copies of the worksheet.

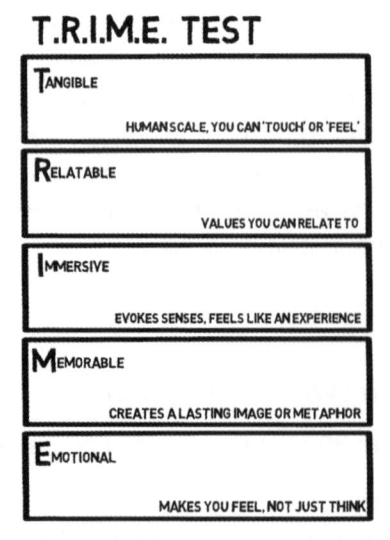

T.R.I.M.E. TEST

TANGIBLE
HUMAN SCALE, YOU CAN 'TOUCH' OR 'FEEL'

RELATABLE
VALUES YOU CAN RELATE TO

IMMERSIVE
EVOKES SENSES, FEELS LIKE AN EXPERIENCE

MEMORABLE
CREATES A LASTING IMAGE OR METAPHOR

EMOTIONAL
MAKES YOU FEEL, NOT JUST THINK

Source: Based on Sachs (2012).

Reflection

How long did you hold people's attention? When did they start to drift off? What kind of questions did they come back with?

References

Sachs, J. (2012) *Winning the Story Wars: Why Those Who Tell – and Live – the Best Stories Will Rule the Future.* Harvard Business School Publishing.
Snyder, B. (2005) *Save the Cat! The Last Book on Screenwriting that You'll Ever Need.* Michael Wiese Productions.
Thomas, D. (2015) Networking workshops: www.davidthomasmedia.com/bizskills

7.7 Hand over the spark

Why

Emotions shape how we see the world and our place in it. They shape our thinking and guide our actions. So if you want to change this world in some way – to create something new – you must consider your emotions and those of the people around you.

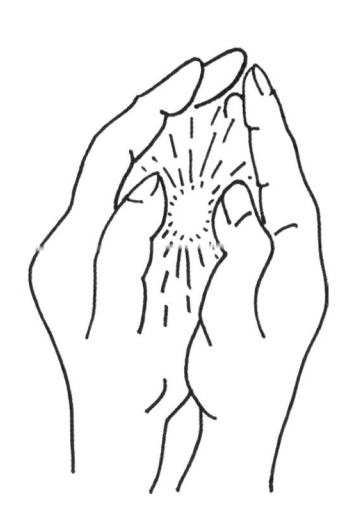

If you want to get other people to help you on the way, then tell them why *you* care. This demands sincerity and a certain amount of vulnerability. You might be thinking, 'This is work, I don't come here to get emotional.' But everything we do has an emotional undercurrent, whether we like it or not.

If you think work is no place to get all touchy-feely, are you actually expressing irritation at your colleagues or perhaps deep pride in your professionalism? What would happen if you played to that positive emotion, rather than trying to leave all emotion out?

Knowledge briefing

Evolutionary psychologists argue that our emotions stem from survival instincts: fears that keep us safe from harm, desires that bond us to our fellow humans. The language we use doesn't just communicate our emotions, it can help shape them too (Watt Smith 2015).

'Emotion determines the meaning of everything,' according to writer Lisa Cron. It gives significance to things and people around us, allowing us to decide what matters and what doesn't (Cron 2012). This matters if we want others to help because 'emotions are mechanisms that set the brain's highest level goals', according to scientist Stephen Pinker (Pinker 1997).

Emotions allow you to 'hand over the spark' of your story, according to screenwriter Bobette Buster. People want to care, they want to be moved, but they are overwhelmed with thousands of messages each day. They need to know why *you* care in order to begin to focus their own emotional radar on *your* message (Buster 2013).

How

1. Try Bobette Buster's story exercises[15]

- Group or solo exercise, 20–30 minutes.

---

[15] Story exercises adapted from Buster (2013).

Big picture

Find the emotions to connect with your audience and hand over your spark of an idea to them:

- What part of your project has moved you or changed the way you see the world?
- How did you feel before you started on this work and how do you feel now? Was there a moment when you 'saw the light'? Describe it and the impact it had on the way you feel.
- Show vulnerability: what are you uncertain about or afraid of? Might your audience feel the same?
- How would you describe your feelings for your project to someone who has never experienced anything like it?

2. Use this book to craft your story

- Solo exercise, 30–40 minutes. You'll need paper and pen.

Look back through the work you've done in the rest of this book.

- Revisit your mission (Chapter 2) – remind yourself why you started out in the first place. Why does it matter? What's at stake? What would the world miss without you?
- Rediscover your insights (Chapter 3) – go back to your 'That's funny . . .' moment. Hook the audience into a detective story as you uncover the clues that led to your insight.
- Recount your motivations (Chapter 3) – how did you discover what was *really* driving people, what they *really* wanted from you?
- Remember the hard work of generating and developing ideas (Chapters 4, 5 and 6) – what were your breakthrough moments? When did it feel like all was lost? How did it all come good in the end?

Reflection

Try your story out on friends and close colleagues. Look for their reactions – where do they lean in and get excited? Ask them the following day what they remember from what you told them. Do they remember what you expected them to, or have they latched onto a different element? Have they picked up on a particular emotion?

References

Buster, B. (2013) *Do/Story: How to Tell Your Story so the World Listens.* The Do Book Company.

Cron, L. (2012) *Wired for Story: The Writer's Guide to Using Brain Science to Hook Readers from the Very First Sentence.* Ten Speed Press.

Pinker. S. (1997) *How the Mind Works.* W.W. Norton.

Watt Smith, T. (2015) *The Book of Human Emotions.* Profile Books.

I wrote this book to help you be creative. You started out looking for new ideas, you built stronger ideas, you threw out bad ideas and now you're here: trying to sell your best ideas to the people who matter most. This is your journey – so how do you feel now?

What did you think of this book?

We're really keen to hear from you about this book, so that we can make our publishing even better.

Please log on to the following website and leave us your feedback.

It will only take a few minutes and your thoughts are invaluable to us.

www.pearsoned.co.uk/bookfeedback

Index

'99 problems' technique 192–3

abstract nouns 238
active inertia 17, 18
active voice 234, 237
algorithms, search 68, 79, 81
Allan, Dave 18, 91, 126, 128, 130, 154, 155–6, 161, 235
amateurs 147, 161
ambiguity
   role 38–9, 56–9
   tolerance for 12–13
analogies 95
analogy springboard 116
analysis-paralysis 20
anomalies 70–1, 84–9, 130
antonyms 242
Apple 161
Argyris, Chris 216
Aristotle 232
art galleries 91
Asimov, Isaac 67
Askildsen, Tormod 41
assumptions 85
   challenging 67, 76–8
   replacing weak 84–6, 88–9
   shaky 158, 159
   testing 38, 54–6, 61
attention, holding 228–9, 250–3
audience, focusing on 223–4, 231–4
autocratic convergent thinking 24
Automated Innovation software 126
autonomy 8, 28, 29
availability heuristic 193
away-days 7, 89–90
   see also field trips

bad ideas 181–2, 189–94
   failing well 186–7, 215–19
   groupthink 183, 199–202
   optimism bias 183–4, 202–5
   overconfidence 184–5, 206–9
   sunk cost fallacy 185–6, 209–15
   the unknown 182, 195–9
bad writing 232–3
Baker, Ralph 55
Barry, Pete 61, 130
basic needs 52, 53–4
Bauer, Jeffrey C. 57, 59
BBC 154, 247
Beatles 82
beginner's mind, adopting 196, 198
Behavioural Insights Team 154, 240
benchmarking 204
Berger, Jonah 243
Berners-Lee, Sir Tim 82
Berra, Yogi 35
best case scenarios 204
beta versions 148
Beveridge, W.I.B. 91
biases
   confirmation 79
   mental shortcuts 182, 185
   optimism 183–4, 202–5
   for safe option 167
   substitution 210
blame 216
Bochner, Stephen 13
Bock, Laszlo 28, 42, 164, 216–17
Booker, Christopher 247
Boyd, Drew 126, 134–6
brain 37, 51, 246
'Brains Trust behaviour' technique 156

Index

Brains Trust, Pixar 154, 156
brainstorming
    avoiding pitfalls of 114
    brainwriting techniques 110–11, 114, 138–41
    breaks 114, 115, 124
    cognitive overload 114
    creative stealing 108–9, 125–9
    divergent thinking 4, 6, 14–16, 20, 21, 22, 26, 30, 107, 120–5
    fixation 114, 115
    free-riders 114
    'inside the box' techniques 110, 133–7
    lateral nudge technique 106–7, 116–18
    lateral thinking 5–6, 17–19, 21, 26, 138, 193–4
    mapping techniques 107–8, 120–5
    metaphor mash technique 106–7, 116, 118–19
    production blocking 114
    rule-breaking techniques 109, 129–33
    rules for 105–6, 113–15
    social matching 114
    wild ideas 114, 115, 149–50, 170–4
'brainwriting sheets' technique 139–40
brainwriting techniques 110–11, 114, 138–41
'break every rule' technique 130–1
Burnette, Charles 190
Buster, Bobette 254–5
Buzan, Tony 120, 121
Bystedt, Jean 91, 95, 97

Cain, Susan 28, 139
capabilities, negative 190, 192
cartoons 95, 96
Catmull, Ed 83, 90, 153, 154, 156, 158, 200
censorship 199, 201
chimp brain 37, 51
cholera 86

Cholle, Francis P. 12
Churchill, Winston 234
Cleese, John 15
cliches 224, 235–6, 238
Coats, Emma 16, 249
cognitive ease 190
cognitive overload, in brainstorming 114
combinatorial creativity 83, 108–9, 125–9
comfort zones 148, 168, 218
commercial confidentiality 160
compatibility of ideas 175, 177
complexity of ideas 175, 177
concept mapping 107, 121, 122–3
confidence 184–5, 206–9
confirmation bias 79
connections, making 69–70, 82–4
contradictions 70–1, 84–9, 130
convergent thinking 6, 20–4, 26, 150–1, 174–8
copying 108, 125, 126
corporate-speak 231–2
creative mission *see* problem definition
creative sessions, planning 28–30
creative stealing 108–9, 125–9
creative thinking 3–4, 11–13
    choosing right tools 9, 31–2
    convergent thinking 6, 20–4, 26, 150–1, 174–8
    divergent thinking 4, 6, 14–16, 20, 21, 22, 26, 30, 107, 120–5
    and group dynamics 8, 27–30
    lateral thinking 5–6, 17–19, 21, 26, 138, 193–4
    testing 12, 13
    time and space for 7, 15, 25–7
critical thinking 167
Cron, Lisa 246, 254
Csikszentmihalyi, Mihaly 83, 85, 126
Cuban missile crisis 199
Cultural Perception Framework 55–6
cultures
    just 216
    workplace 83, 85, 157, 216
curators 81

Index

daily development meetings 158–9
Darwin, Charles 120
Davies, Stephanie 28, 75–6
daydreaming mode 26
de Bono, Edward 17–18, 130
Deacon, Terrence 116
dead verbs 238
deadlines for developing ideas 154, 156
democratic convergent thinking 22–3
design thinking 147–8, 163–6
developer's dilemma 145, 153
developing ideas 145–6, 153–7
    deadlines 154, 156
    design thinking 147–8, 163–6
    final approval of ideas 150–1, 174–8
    keeping novelty alive 148–9, 166–70, 174
    open innovation 147, 160–3
    supportive teams 146, 157–60
    wild ideas 149–50, 170–4
development hell 154
development meetings, daily 158–9
development teams 146, 157–60
devil's advocate technique 114, 200, 201–2
Diehl, Michael 138
direct questions 73, 95
Disney, Walt 120
distractions 25–6, 92
divergent thinking 4, 6, 14–16, 20, 21, 22, 26, 30, 107, 120–5
Don't Tell the Bride 76–7
dot-voting systems 23, 46, 122, 141
doubt 190, 192
D'Souza, Steven 190, 192, 196
Duncan, Kevin 116
Dweck, Carol 216, 218

Eberle, Bob 134, 136–7
elephant-in-the-room problems 49
elevator pitches 251–2
emotional gifting 243, 244
emotional messages 251, 252
emotions 99, 100
    and messages 243, 251, 252, 253–6

and motivation 72–3, 94–7
    negative 190
errors *see* bad ideas; failures
escape hatches 167–8, 169
ethos 232, 233
euphemisms 232
'eureka!' 67, 75
evolutionary psychology 254
executive brain 37, 51
expert forecasters 206, 207–8
extroverts 28, 29

facilitators 30
fail fast philosophy 148
failures
    and design thinking 147–8, 163–6
    learning from 186–7, 215–19
    thoughtful 164, 165
fear 51, 53, 190, 254
    of the unknown 182
feedback 208
field notes 92, 93, 97
field trips 71–2, 89–93, 97
filter bubbles 68–9, 78–81
Firestien, Roger 45, 48, 167, 168–9, 175
'five whys' technique 36, 44–7, 49–50
fixation, in brainstorming 114, 115
fixed mindset 216
'floor-walking' technique 140–1
Flyvbjerg, Bent 204
forecasting
    expert forecasters 206, 207–8
    reference class 204
    superforecasters 207, 209
'four ways of seeing' technique 38, 54–6
free-riders, in brainstorming 114
freshness stores 71–2, 90, 91–2
FUN technique 173–4, 178
functional ideas 173–4
future scenarios 96

Galilei, Galileo 84
Gallo, Carmine 60, 239, 246
Gardner, Daniel 207
Geschka, Horst 139

Index

Gettins, Dominic 236, 237–8
give and take matrix 38–9, 56–9
goal compass 43–4, 62–3
goal insights 158, 159
Goldenberg, Jacob 126, 134–6
good ideas *see* developing ideas; selling ideas
Google 28, 42, 164, 216–17
Gray, David 21–2, 58, 131–2
'greenhouse behaviour' technique 155–6
Grivas, Chris 12, 157
group dynamics 8, 27–30
group morality 201
group size 29
groupthink 183, 199–202
growth mindset 216, 218
Guilford, J.P. 12
Gunning Fog Index 228, 251, 252
gut instincts 48, 148, 151
Gutenberg, Johannes 82

Hague, Paul 95
Halligan, Peter 116
Halpern, David 154
Hammond, Claudia 52
'hedgehogs and foxes' 207, 208
Heffernan, Margaret 90–1, 210, 215, 216
Hemingway, Ernest 239–40
Hertz, Noreena 26
heuristic ideation technique 134
heuristics 134, 193
hierarchy of needs 52
hindsight 18
hooks, crafting compelling 73–4, 98–102
'how could we . . . ?' questions 46–7, 48, 166, 168
humble ground rules 211
humility 190, 192
humour 75–6
hypocrisy 98

Iannucci, Armando 206
icebreakers 29

ideas *see* bad ideas; brainstorming; developing ideas; selling ideas
illusion of invulnerability 201
illusion of unanimity 201
images 116
'imagine a world without you' technique 35, 41–4
immersive messages 251, 252
imposter syndrome 232
indirect questions 73, 95–6
information sources, diversifying 68–9, 78–81
innovation checklist 177, 178
'inside the box' techniques 110, 133–7
insights 67–8, 75–8
  and contradictions 70–1, 84–9
  crafting hooks from 73–4, 98–102
  discovering motivations 72–3, 94–7
  diversifying information sources 68–9, 78–81
  field trips 71–2, 89–93, 97
  goal 158, 159
  making connections 69–70, 82–4
inspiration *see* brainstorming
intellectual property 160
internet
  creativity tests 13
  open innovation 147, 160–3
  readability tests 228–9, 251, 252
  search algorithms 68, 79, 81
  testing ideas 164
  viral messages 226–7, 242–5
introverts 28, 29, 111, 139
invulnerability, illusion of 201
Iraq War 55, 195
irony 74, 98–102
Ito, Joi 164, 196

Janis, Irving 199, 200–1
jargon 223, 234
Jaws 99
Jobs, Steve 82
Johnson, Steven 83, 126, 161
just cultures 216

Index

'just give me a sign!' technique 193–4

Kahn, Robert L. 57
Kahneman, Daniel 18, 48, 79, 130, 190, 193, 196, 203, 204, 207, 210, 217, 239, 240
Kersting, Karen 171
King, Zella 79
Klein, Gary 75, 85, 126, 158, 167–8, 203–4, 207
Kleon, Austin 126
Kohn, Nicholas 113
Kolko, Jon 164
Kremer, William 52

'laddering' techniques 95, 96–7
lateral nudge technique 106–7, 116–18
lateral thinking 5–6, 17–19, 21, 26, 138, 193–4
Lawrence, Paul 52
Leadbeater, Charles 161
LEGO 41–2, 160, 161, 162, 175
LEGO innovation matrix technique 176–7
lessons learned
 failing well 186–7, 215–19
 reframing losses as 186, 210, 211–15
Levitin, Daniel 12, 26
lightbulb moments 26
live testing 148, 164
lizard brain 37, 51
'lizard, the chimp and business exec' technique 37, 51–4
logic and reason 37, 48
logos 232, 233
Lois, George 91
long words 234, 238
loss aversion 185–6, 210–11
losses, reframing as lessons learned 186, 210, 211–15
Lynch, Clare 237–8

McCaffrey, Anthony 126, 128
magazines 92–3

Mango phone 136
mapping techniques 107–8, 120–5
market research 71, 73, 94, 95
Marshall, Hazel 247
Maslow, Abraham 3, 52
MediaCityUK 154
memorable messages 251, 252
mental models 200
mental shortcuts 182, 185
messages
 holding attention 228–9, 250–3
 readability tests 228–9, 251, 252
 real, original and simple 224–5, 235–8
 reframing 225, 226, 240, 241–2
 rhetorical devices 225–6, 239–42
 road-testing 228–9, 250–3
 storytelling 227–8, 246–9
 structuring 223–4, 231–4
 viral 226–7, 242–5
metaphor mash technique 106–7, 116, 118–19
metaphors 116, 236
military theorists 55, 196, 200, 203–4
Miller, Blair 165
mind-guards, self-appointed 199, 201
mind mapping 107, 120–2
Mindstorms 161
mirroring 55
mission *see* problem definition
'mission impossible' technique 131–2
mission statements 36, 39–40, 45–7, 60–3
mistakes *see* bad ideas; failures
MIT Media Lab 164, 196
modes of thought 26
Monty Python 15
mood 190, 192
motivations 72–3, 94–7
Motorola 136
Mueller, Jennifer S. 21, 167, 171
multiple maps 123–4
museums 91, 92

naive experts 161
Natural History Unit, BBC 247

261

Index

needs
  basic 52, 53–4
  hierarchy of 52
negative capabilities 190, 192
negative emotions 190
networks *see* social networks
new ideas 173–4
New Scientist 116
New York Times 243
Newton, Isaac 120
Nike 160
Noria, Nitin 52
nouns
  abstract 238
  as verbs 238
Novak, Joseph D. 121
novelty, keeping alive 21, 24, 139–40, 148–9, 166–70, 174

observability of ideas 175, 177
Ogilvy, David 234
omission 225–6, 239–40, 241
online communities 147, 160, 161, 162
online creativity tests 13
online readability tests 228–9, 251, 252
open-ended questions 36–7, 48–50, 159, 167, 168–70
open innovation 147, 160–3
open-minded groups 201
optimism bias 183–4, 202–5
organ donors 240
organisational cultures 83, 85, 157, 216
original messages 224, 235–7
Orwell, George 234, 235–7, 238
Osborn, Alex 170–1
outsider views 204–5
overconfidence 184–5, 206–9

Page, Scott E. 15, 160
parentheses 237
Pariser, Eli 79
Parnes, Sidney J. 45
passive voice 234, 237
Passuello, Luciano 192
pathos 232, 233
patience 190, 192

patterns
  and lateral thinking 5, 17–19
  repetition in threes 225, 239, 240
Paulus, Paul B. 139
people-watching 91, 92, 93
persuasive arguments 232, 233
pin-boards 93
Pink, Daniel H. 28
Pinker, Stephen 254
Pixar 16, 83, 90, 153, 154, 156, 158, 200, 249
plagiarism 108, 125, 126
planning fallacy 204
playing it safe 21, 114, 148, 149, 167
'pluses, potentials and concerns (PPC)' technique 168–9
post-mortems 207, 209, 217–18
Poynton, Robert 153
PPC *see* 'pluses, potentials and concerns (PPC)' technique
practically valuable ideas 244
prairie fires 86
praise 218
pre-mortem analysis 203–4, 205
pro-am producers 161
problem definition
  'five whys' technique 36, 44–7, 49–50
  'four ways of seeing' technique 38, 54–6
  give and take matrix 38–9, 56–9
  'imagine a world without you' technique 35, 41–4
  'lizard, the chimp and business exec' technique 37, 51–4
  reframing problems 36–7, 47–50
  'tweet simplicity' technique 39–40, 60–3, 240
problem matrices 191–2
production blocking, in brainstorming 114
projective questions 95–6
prototyping 147–8, 164, 165–6, 235, 236
Puccio, Gerard J. 12, 20, 21, 157, 165

questions
  direct 73, 95

Index

'five whys' technique 36, 44–7, 49–50
'how could we . . . ?' 46–7, 48, 166, 168
indirect 73, 95–6
open-ended 36–7, 48–50, 159, 167, 168–70
projective 95–6
responding with 157, 159, 167, 168–70

RAIN thinking 155
Raphaelson, Joel 232
re-expression technique 126, 128
readability tests 228–9, 251, 252
real messages 224, 235, 236
real-world experiences 71–2, 89–93
reason and logic 37, 48
Red Team tools 55
reference class forecasting 204
reframing
  losses as lessons learned 186, 210, 211–15
  messages 225, 226, 240, 241–2
  problems 36–7, 48–50
rehearsal loops 12
relatable messages 251, 252
relative advantage of ideas 175, 177
Renner, Diana 190, 192, 196
repetition in threes 225, 239, 240
reptilian brain 37, 51
reputation management 160
resilience 216
rhetorical devices 225–6, 239–42
risk tolerance 190–1
road-testing
  ideas 165, 236
  messages 228–9, 250–3
Robertson, David 42, 161, 162, 175, 176–7
Robinson, Sir Ken 15
Robson, Sir Bobby 5
Roche 160
Rogers, Everett M. 175, 177, 178
role ambiguity 38–9, 56–9
role play 95, 96, 236
Roman, Kenneth 232
Rowlands, Jon 76–7

rule-breaking techniques 109, 129–33
Rumsfeld, Donald 195

Sachs, Jonah 246, 251, 252
sadness 190
safe options 21, 114, 148, 149, 167
sarcasm 98
SCAMPER technique 134, 136–7
Schulz, Kathryn 210
scriptwriting technique 74
search algorithms 68, 79, 81
self-appointed mind-guards 199, 201
self-censorship 199, 201
Selfe, Carl 123
selling ideas
  focusing on audience 223–4, 231–4
  handing over the spark 229–30, 253–6
  holding attention 228–9, 250–3
  real, original and simple messages 224–5, 235–8
  rhetorical devices 225–6, 239–42
  road-testing messages 228–9, 250–3
  storytelling 227–8, 246–9
  structuring messages 223–4, 231–4
  viral messages 226–7, 242–5
senior leaders 28, 30
sentence structure 251
shaky assumptions 158, 159
sharing persona 243
short words 234, 238
show and tell 96
signpost and yardstick 62
silence 190, 192
silent working 29, 111, 114, 138–41
Simmons, Peter R. 57, 59
Simonton, Dean Keith 121, 171
Simple Measure of Gobbledegook (SMOG) 228, 251
simplifying messages 225, 234, 236, 237–8
'tweet simplicity' technique 39–40, 60–3, 240
sincerity 254
single-minded benefit 61

263

Index

six-step storyboard 249
slow hunches 83
Smith, Steven M. 113
SMOG (Simple Measure of Gobbledegook) 228, 251
Snow, John 86
Snyder, Blake 98, 251
social matching, in brainstorming 114
social networks
  as information sources 79, 81
  making connections 69–70, 82–4
solar system 84
'steal from a thesaurus' technique 128
'steal from the heart' technique 108–9, 125–7
stealing, creative 108–9, 125–9
Stevens, Michael 243
story arcs 248
story exercises 254–5
storyboard, six-step 249
storytelling 227–8, 246–9
Stroebe, Wolfgang 138
substitutes 236
substitution bias 210
'subtraction' technique 134–6
suggestions boxes 169
Sull, Donald N. 18
SUN thinking 155, 156
sunk cost fallacy 185–6, 209–15
sunset clauses 154, 156
Sunstein, Cass 203
superforecasters 207, 209
supportive teams 146, 157–60
Surowiecki, James 160
survival instincts 254
symbols 116
synonyms 128
system 1 thinking 48
system 2 thinking 48

Taleb, Nassim Nicholas 91, 196, 208
tangible messages 251, 252
task negative thinking 26
task positive thinking 26
Taster (BBC) 154

Tauber, Edward M. 134
team-working 113–14
teams
  development 146, 157–60
  group dynamics 8, 27–30
Tetlock, Philip 207
Thaler, Richard 203
'that's funny . . .' 67–8, 75–8
theories, rewriting current 84–8
thesauruses 128, 242
thinking
  convergent 6, 20–4, 26, 150–1, 174–8
  critical 167
  design 147–8, 163–6
  divergent 4, 6, 14–16, 20, 21, 22, 26, 30, 107, 120–5
  lateral 5–6, 17–19, 21, 26, 138, 193–4
  outside the box 133–4
  system 1 and system 2 48
  see also creative thinking
Thomas, David 251
thoughtful failures 164, 165
threes, repetition in 225, 239, 240
time and space for creative thinking 7, 15, 25–7
Toyota 44
Treasure, Julian 239
trialability of ideas 175, 177
tricolons 225, 239, 240
TRIME test 251, 252
Tversky, Amos 204
'tweet simplicity' technique 39–40, 60–3, 240
Twitter 60

UK government 154, 240
unanimity, illusion of 201
uncertainty 21, 167
  role ambiguity 38–9, 56–9
  tolerance for 12–13
unexpected ideas 173–4
University of Foreign Military and Cultural Studies 55, 196, 197–8, 200, 203–4
the unknown 182, 195–9

US Patent Office 171
useless maps metaphor 196

verbs
  dead 238
  nouns as 238
viral messages 226–7, 242–5
vulnerability 254, 255

Wallace, Amy 83, 90, 154, 158, 200
Watt Smith, Tiffany 254
weak ties 79, 81
Weich, John 247
'what if?' analysis 196, 197–8
?WhatIf! creative agency 153, 155–6
'what's your problem?' technique 48–50

wild ideas 114, 115, 149–50, 170–4
'wisdom of the crowd' theory 160–1
Woolard, Adrian 154
word associations 95
word length 234, 238, 251
workload imbalances 38, 58–9
workplace cultures 83, 85, 157, 216
worst-case scenarios 204, 205
writing 12, 29
  bad 232–3
  see also messages
Wuchty, Stefan 114

Yang, Huei-Chuan 139

Zenasni, Franck 12